Supporting Independent Readers:

Instructional Strategies to
Increase Proficiency and Engagement

Supporting Independent Readers:

Instructional Strategies to Increase Proficiency and Engagement

Nancy Allison
Spring Woods Middle School
Houston, Texas

Christopher-Gordon Publishers, Inc.
Norwood, Massachusetts

Copyright Acknowledgments

Every effort has been made to contact copyright holders for permission to reproduce borrowed material where necessary. We apologize for any oversights and would be happy to rectify them in future printings.

Copyright © 2007 by Christopher-Gordon Publishers, Inc.

All rights reserved. Except for review purposes, no part of this material protected by this copyright notice may be reproduced or utilized in any form or by any means, electronic or mechanical, including photocopying, recording, or any information and retrieval system, without the express written permission of the publisher or copyright holder.

Christopher~Gordon Publishers, Inc.
Bridging Theory and Practice

1502 Providence Highway, Suite 12
Norwood, MA 02062

800-934-8322 • 781-762-5577
www.Christopher-Gordon.com

Printed in the United State of America
10 9 8 7 6 5 4 3 2 1   09 08 07

ISBN: 1-933760-07-9
Library of Congress Catalogue Number: 2006936460

Table of Contents

Dedication ix

Acknowledgments xi

Preface xiii

Chapter 1: Re-Viewing Independent Reading 1
    Activity versus instruction 1
    A different vision 3
    What is independence? 3
    Supported independent reading in the balanced literacy classroom .. 4
    The teacher's role in supported independent reading 6
    The first essential of supported independent reading:
        self-selected texts 7
    The second essential of supported independent reading:
        choosing to grow 10
    Setting the stage for finding books in the library 12
    Preparing for the unexpected 14
    Dealing with poor choices 15
    The third essential: teacher monitoring and intervention 16
    References 17
        Trade books cited 18

Chapter 2: Providing Structures for Growth 19
    The structure of supported independent reading 20
    Teacher responsibilities 21

The classroom library	21
Reading logs	27
Teaching expectations	28
The minilesson	30
A sample minilesson on summarization	31
Targeted conferencing	33
Taking conference notes	34
Time for response	35
The adventure of teaching	35
References	36

Chapter 3: Engaging Readers 37

Redefining the term *reader*	38
A lesson to build the concept of *reader*	38
Teaching for engagement	42
Previous reading experiences	43
Expectations for reading	44
A series of lessons aimed at changing expectations	45
The classroom culture	50
References	52
Trade books cited	52

Chapter 4: Organized Note Taking: A Tool for Making Thought Visible 55

Developing the abilities for response	56
The reality of reading instruction	56
Keeping the focus on reading	57
Organized note taking	57
Choosing the target	58
Notes, not worksheets	59
A week of skill-related responses	60
Creating responses	63
Talk as a response	64
A brief word about accountability	64
References	65

Chapter 5: Deskside Conferencing: A Launchpad for Growth 67

What is deskside conferencing?	69
Preparing for the conference	70
What kinds of things are taught in a deskside conference?	70

One reader at a time	71
The teacher's deskside manner	73
The purpose and structure of a conference	73
Initiating the conference	74
Assessing the responses	75
Sharpening the focus of the conference and offering advice that guides	75
Checking for understanding	79
Knowing the readers through conferencing	80
References	80
Trade books cited	81

Chapter 6: Conferencing with Delayed Readers 83
- Understanding the delayed reader 84
- The behaviors of delayed readers 85
- Reducing the threat of reading 86
- Conferencing with a helpless reader 86
- A conference with a smoke and mirrors reader 90
- A conference with a starving reader 94
- Getting delayed readers on their way 96
- Common teaching points in conferences with delayed readers 97
  - General reading hints 97
  - Fiction texts 97
  - Nonfiction texts 98
- References 99
  - Trade books cited 99

Chapter 7: Conferencing with On-Level Readers 101
- The needs of on-level readers 102
- A conference with a book trader 103
- A conference with a page turner 106
- Remembering our on-level readers 107
- Common teaching points in conferences with on-level readers 108
  - General reading hints 108
  - Fiction texts 108
  - Nonfiction texts 109
- References 110
  - Trade books cited 110

Chapter 8: Conferencing with Gifted Readers 111
    A conference with a speeding reader 112
    A conference with a lingering reader 115
    Common teaching points in conferences with gifted readers 117
        General reading hints 117
        Fiction texts 117
        Nonfiction texts 118
    References 118
        Trade books cited 119

Appendix A 121
Appendix B 123
Appendix C 124
Appendix D 125
Appendix E 127
Appendix F 128
Appendix G 129
Appendix H 130
Appendix I 131
Appendix J 132

References 133

Index 139

About the Author 143

Dedication

*This book is dedicated to
all the teachers for whom
teaching a love of reading
is an essential
educational objective.*

Acknowledgments

I often feel like I live a charmed life. I have been blessed with a wonderful family and supportive, encouraging friends throughout my life and career. Without the constant push of people telling me I needed to write a book, this one would never have happened.

Thanks first of all to Dr. Lee Mountain, who really gave me no choice but to write. She is an amazing support to all who know her and are privileged to work with her on publishing. Thank you for all the e-mails and phone calls. Novice writers can learn so much from you—and you are never too busy to listen.

I graduated from college more years ago than I care to admit and got a secondary certification, so I took *no* reading classes at all. But again I was blessed when, 12 years ago, Dr. Judy Wallis entered my life. When I was a brand-new language arts specialist who knew a lot about writing and nothing about reading, she believed in me and steered me to all the right books and all the right ideas. Judy shaped my thinking and beliefs about reading instruction, and her continued guidance and counsel helps me grow every day. Judy is who I want to be when I grow up.

During the 2005–2006 school year, a master teacher named Mikaela Van de Water agreed to take a group of students who had failed our state's assessment as half of her 50-student team. She then allowed me to coteach with her throughout the school year, an experience I will always treasure. Although pseudonyms are used throughout this book, the students in it are very real—and most of them came from Mikaela's classroom. I cannot thank her enough for allowing me to work with her, for trying a new concept, for being the incredibly insightful and compassionate teacher that she is, and for being my friend.

To all the teachers at Budewig Intermediate School in Alief ISD who believed me when I told them supported independent reading would work, I owe a huge debt. The 3 years I spent working with such consummate professionals who were willing to take risks and try something new will inspire me for years to come. Thanks to each of you for educating children so amazingly well.

I am so grateful to two of my dearest friends for their constant pressure on me to do more and to be more. Thanks to Ann Malone, the world's all-time best principal. She sets a standard for leadership by valuing teachers and their opinions and by fighting for their right to make well-thought-out professional decisions that will positively impact children. She also sets a standard for living by enjoying work and play with equal enthusiasm. Thanks also go to Lynn Bullard—who takes no excuses. Her strength of character, her incredible wit, and her unwavering friendship add to my life every day. What a blessing to have such friends.

And to my family—thank you for tolerating the makeshift desk near the TV, the stacks of books on the floor, and the irritated complaints when my train of thought was interrupted. I know you are proud of this book; *I* am proud to be part of each of your lives. Each of you shows me every day what strength of character truly means. With the examples of your lives, each one of you reminds me that there is no obstacle that cannot be overcome with faith, love, and determination. So my deepest thanks to Harry, Jennifer, Susan, Allie, Joe (#76), Ross, and Lola. Without your total support and understanding, this book would never have come to be.

Preface

Reading is a hard sell in today's society. In a world where 40-hour work weeks are rare, where homes are wired for over a hundred television channels that broadcast 24 hours a day, where organized sports teams exist for people from ages 3 to 103, and where 24-hour gyms dangle fit and attractive lifestyles in front of us all, sitting quietly lost in a book seems an old-fashioned thing to do.

In addition to this, many of the students with whom I work live in poverty in neighborhoods where it is not safe to be outside day or night. Most of their parents work two jobs or work on the nightshift—and these young people are often left unsupervised after school. The presence of video games and cable TV in their homes is a financial sacrifice their parents have made to try and keep their children safe inside their own homes. Because they have not been blessed with strong reading role models, they have not yet learned that reading is an adventure and a joy that could also keep their children safe.

To further complicate their relationship with reading, many of these students have been below level in their reading skills since they entered pre-K not knowing the alphabet or numbers or how to write their names. Well-meaning teachers have chosen all their books and structured all their reading time with the consistent goal of teaching them what "good readers" do. They aren't good readers—and they know it. They see the instruction as something aimed at students different from themselves.

In this age of accountability, it is easy to lose sight of the fact that the best readers are the ones who read the most. Our instruction needs to target both skills and engagement if we are to lead our most challenged students to success.

This book is built on the premise that there needs to be a layer of instruction between guided reading and independent reading that offers support to students as they begin to tackle texts on their own. During supported independent reading, students should be engaged with books that they themselves have chosen while the teacher travels through the room conducting one-on-one conferences with readers engaged in the act of reading. This powerful instructional strategy can lead students both to reading proficiency and to a lifelong love of reading.

Chapter 1 separates supported independent reading from other views of independent reading and explains this strategy's place in a balanced literacy program. It also lays out both teacher and student responsibilities and the essentials for success with this important instructional configuration, including specific suggestions on how to help students self-select texts that are right for them.

Chapter 2 gives an overview of each of the components of a supported independent reading program, with special emphasis on the minilesson and on taking conference notes.

An entire chapter is devoted to reading engagement in chapter 3. The truth is that unless students are engaged with the texts they are reading, the time spent in independent reading is wasted. Sample lessons are provided based on McKenna's research on literacy motivation.

Chapter 4 discusses readers' responses to supported independent reading, where the emphasis should be on reading skills rather than on writing. Graphic organizers are recommended for response, and an entire week's worth of lessons are given as samples to show how the work done during response builds on the teaching done previously and also gives the teacher an insight to student mastery of targeted skills and strategies.

Since deskside conferencing is the teaching piece of supported independent reading, the rest of the book deals with conferencing in detail. Chapter 5 explains the structure and purpose of these conferences, including suggested conference starters and responses. Chapters 6–8 then deal with specific issues encountered when working with delayed, on-level, and gifted readers. Each chapter gives an overview of these types of readers, several actual classroom conferences for each, and common teaching points for each.

I believe that reading teachers still have a true desire to instill a love of reading in their students but often feel limited by the demands of high-stakes testing and accountability. With supported independent reading, students can score well on tests *and* learn to love reading. A reading teacher could never ask for more.

Chapter 1

Re-Viewing Independent Reading

Independent reading is a powerful instructional tool that seldom reaches its full potential. In this age of accountability and balanced literacy, it is the independent reading piece that is the most misunderstood and poorly implemented. Intermediate- and middle school students are still learning to read—and meeting them at the point of their confusions to help them clarify their thinking can result in great gains both in learning and in proficiency. However, when teachers view independent reading time as time for students to work alone, valuable teachable moments are lost.

In the building where I teach, independent reading is the heart of the reading program. Ask the teachers, and they'll tell you it is a critical instructional piece that leads not only to the creation of lifelong readers, but also to higher standardized test scores. By spending 30 minutes each day reading independently in self-selected texts with teacher support, students build stamina and increase their background knowledge of texts and the world. Instead of *learning* about reading, they are actually *doing* it.

Activity Versus Instruction

Recently, a controversial decision in a neighboring district mandated that the teachers there use a basal reader for instruction. The "independent reading" piece of the program called for the students to read small books that could be read in one sitting and that were written to reinforce the skills and vocabulary on which the week's lesson focused. When told of this change, a principal I know, who has long been an advocate for a strong independent reading program, looked at the central office administrator who was delivering the message and asked, "But when are the kids supposed to read in books that they've chosen themselves from the library?"

The administrator's answer: They could read those in the hallways during bathroom breaks—or in the cafeteria during breakfast and lunch.

Clearly, the central office administrator's view of independent reading and mine are very different. If she envisions it as something the students do outside of instructional time to keep them occupied, she sees independent reading as an activity. Yes, it might actually support the curriculum, but since no more knowledgeable other (Vygotsky, 1978) is monitoring the learning, it is not instruction. Apparently, that is one point on which the administrator and I would agree—independent reading that is not monitored by the teacher so that students can have assistance at the point of confusion belongs in the cafeteria during breakfast and in the hallway during bathroom breaks.

Instruction, on the other hand, implies that someone—namely, the teacher—is actually helping the learner learn. According to Vygtosky (1978), student growth occurs when instruction is given in what he calls the zone of proximal development, an area of difficulty just above what the student can do alone. In this zone, a more knowledgeable other is needed to support the learning with the goal of making the child able to work at this same level without assistance. Any activities designed to be completed totally independently should, therefore, be at levels *below* this essential learning zone. These, then, are activities—not instruction—meant to reinforce what has already been learned, not to create new learning.

This is why the currently popular views of independent reading trigger a lack of respect. In most classrooms, independent reading is viewed in one of two ways: as a time for the teacher to read along with the students as a model of reading (the sustained silent reading [SSR] model) or as an activity to keep students busy while the teacher pulls a small guided reading group. To the teacher devoted to SSR as a model, independent reading is reading done for pleasure during the school day for which students are not held accountable in any way. To the teacher who pulls small groups during this time, independent reading is time set aside for students to read in books below their zone of proximal development for which they are held accountable through reading logs and responses. Each downgrades independent reading to an activity and removes it from the realm of true instruction.

Independent reading should be more productive than this. In each of these configurations, time that should be used for instruction is instead used by the majority of the students as time to complete *activities* alone. The students might as well be somewhere outside of school during this time—a teacher is apparently optional.

A Different Vision

Consider a different concept of independent reading, one in which the teacher is actively working with students who are reading books they themselves have chosen.

In this view, the teacher works the room, moving from student to student to assess instructional needs and offering just the right guidance at just the right time to help students grow. Teachers are *teaching* during this time, but their lessons are springing from the needs of the students as they work individually, which is very different from leaving them to work alone. Although both Calkins (2001) and Fountas and Pinnell (2001) advocate conferencing during independent reading, this piece of literacy instruction is often overlooked as teachers busy themselves with other activities while students read unmonitored.

What Is Independence?

Both of my daughters are grown and have been living "independently" for several years. As they were growing up, my husband and I worked hard at trying to guide them to be self-sufficient adults who would be equipped to live the kind of lives they envisioned for themselves. But they still call for advice on things like what to do about my granddaughter's earache or which job offer seems the most promising. They will independently make these decisions—but they still want us to share some of what we have learned from having more years of experience.

Being a teacher is not that different from being a parent. As students grow as readers, the teacher must try to guide their development, aiming always to make them self-sufficient and able to tackle any reading task before them. The teacher is still the one with more years of experience—and there will still be times when students will need to ask for advice or when it will be offered at a time of need.

Just as individuals choose the direction of their lives, students should choose the direction of their reading. They should pursue their interests and be excited about the reading paths they have chosen. But teachers must also realize that these developing readers will still need guidance—even if they aren't always aware of that fact.

Different students will present different challenges. The boy who's read only graphic novels will need help learning to use the words on the page to make pictures in his mind. The girl who has read every *Ramona Quimby* book will need help adjusting to texts with new sets of characters. The boy who is confused about events in his first science fiction novel will need guidance as he learns to stretch his imagination. These students should be encouraged to challenge themselves and to try to do things on their own. But if they encounter difficulty, the teacher should be available to help them, not off in a corner reading a book or leading a small group that they are not allowed to interrupt. If someone is not there to notice the confusions and frustrations as they occur, these students will probably give up and return to the texts that are comfortable for them. They will be comfortable—but they will not grow as readers.

Independence, then, should be both encouraged and supported. There will be students who only need the teacher to touch base with them every couple of days as they immerse themselves in books such as Paolini's (2005) *Eldest* and Jacques's (1988) *Mossflower*. Their support will be quite different from students who continually abandon books or who have never read a chapter book all the way through. But if they do hit a rough spot, they will know from watching the teacher work with the readers around them that someone will be there to help them, too. This is the power of supported independent reading.

Supported Independent Reading in the Balanced Literacy Classroom

Imagine a pebble being dropped into still water. Picture how the waves would spread in concentric circles out from the pebble into the stillness. The circles would get larger and the waves smaller the farther the water was from the pebble itself, until finally the water would become still again.

In a balanced literacy classroom, instruction spreads out in similar circles, with the teacher serving as the catalyst. The tighter circles near the center require more of the teacher's control (Fig. 1:1). As the circles grow wider, the teacher releases more and more of the responsibility for the task to the individual readers themselves in what Gallagher and Pearson (1983) have called the gradual release of responsibility. And at the far edge, out where the learning waters are still, is independent work in literacy centers or work stations where students keep skills sharp by practicing what they already know and another layer of reading that can be called personal reading—reading students choose to do on their own in texts they have chosen for their own purposes. These are the activities students can do without teacher intervention.

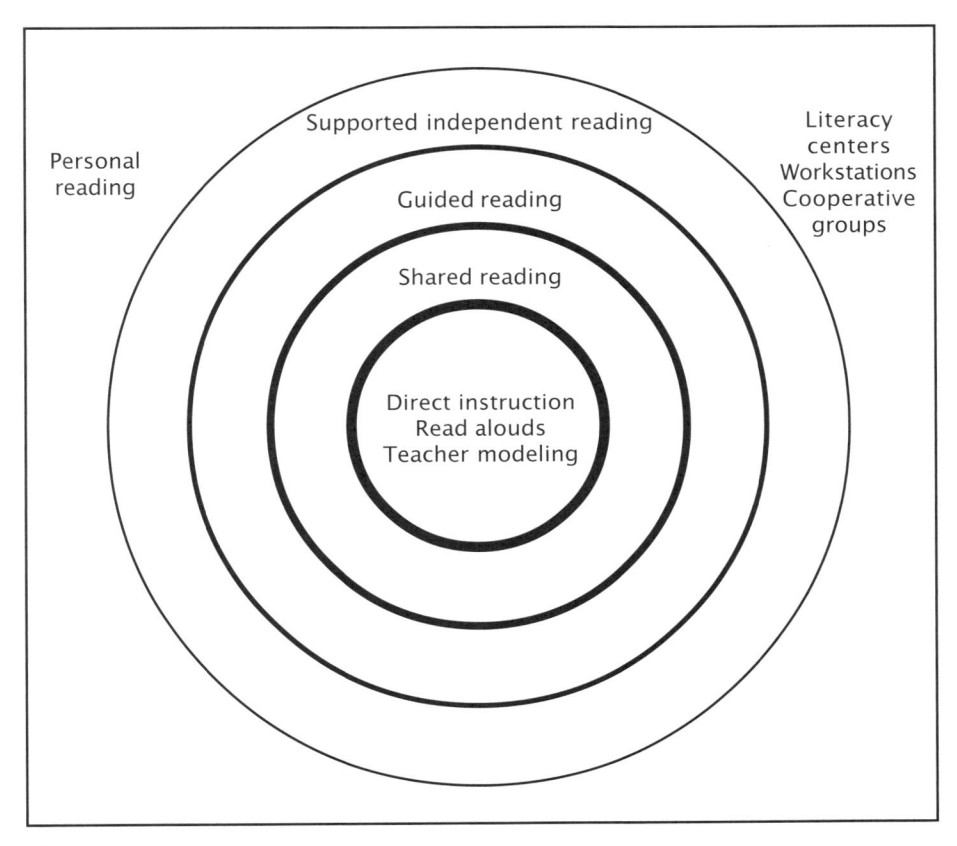

Figure 1:1 Levels of teacher support.

There are basically four elements whose control can be negotiated in an instructional reading experience: the text, the decoding, the focus, and the application of skills and strategies. When skills or strategies are introduced, the teacher controls all four elements: choosing a text that fits the lesson's focus, reading it aloud, and applying the skills or strategies while students watch and learn.

In shared reading, the teacher continues to control the text and set the focus. The decoding workload is minimized by having the teacher or another capable reader read the text aloud. Students are encouraged to apply the skill or strategy being taught, but the teacher steps in and takes control at points of confusion.

In guided reading, the teacher relinquishes responsibility for decoding but continues to choose the text and the focus for reading. Application of the target skills or strategies during guided reading is assessed, and students are prompted, as necessary, to help them apply them on their own.

The traditional balanced literacy model moves from guided to independent reading, but there needs to be a level between these two instructional configurations in which the developing reader works with the *support* rather than the *guidance* of the teacher. When students are *guided*, the teacher is out in front of them, pulling them along a path the teacher has selected. When they are *supported*, however, the implication is that students are in the lead and someone is behind them helping them accomplish a task they themselves have chosen. This level of instruction is supported independent reading.

The older the students are, the more time should be devoted to supported independent reading. Unlike math, where new skills are introduced in a sequential manner, reading is more of a global exercise. Once students reach the intermediate grades, where the focus shifts from decoding to comprehension, it is essential that students be given the chance to practice in a situation that more clearly mimics the reading they will do in the "real world."

The reading curriculum for fourth grade does not differ that much from the curriculum for eighth grade—the difference is the complexity of the texts in which the students are expected to apply these skills. Students will have been exposed to several years of skill lessons before they reach the intermediate grades and middle school, so most of the students will not need as much in-depth teaching of these skills as younger students might as they explore them for the first time. Instead, these older students will need more time to apply these skills in more sophisticated texts. Time spent on supported independent reading should increase and time spent on more teacher-directed activities should decrease as the students' skills advance. The goal, after all, is student independence.

The Teacher's Role in Supported Independent Reading

The teacher's only role in supported independent reading is to check in with readers as they work on their own and to support them when areas of confusion are identified. Individual readers may need help not only with skills and strategies that have been studied by the whole class or the small group, but also with challenges they encounter on their own which may not have been addressed in other instruction. Sometimes, the teacher will identify these areas for growth, and sometimes the focus of the conference will be determined by the questions the readers have.

Supported independent reading is similar to guided reading (Fig. 1:2) but gives control of the text, the decoding, the focus, and the application over to the students. In both instructional configurations, the teacher is there to assist students as they try to decode and to apply skills and strategies independently. Deskside conferences during supported independent reading, however, meet the students' needs, not the teacher's. The students are in control—but, much like training wheels, the teacher is there to help steady them should they wobble and appear ready to fall.

Supported independent reading, then, is reading done in mostly self-selected texts written at appropriate levels to spur growth, in which the actual reading of the texts is monitored by a teacher who intervenes, as necessary, to insure success.

Guided Reading	Supported Independent Reading
Usually involves 4-6 students working with the teacher	Involves the teacher working one-on-one with students
Text is chosen by the teacher	Text is chosen by the student with teacher guidance as needed
Focus of the instruction is predetermined by the teacher and is the same for every member of the group	Focus is determined by student responses and behaviors during a one-on-one conference and is individualized
Focuses teacher attention on a small group for 15-30 minutes while other students work alone	Focuses teacher attention on all students as needs arise
Students are expected to do the decoding work and apply targeted skills and strategies with teacher support	Students are expected to do the decoding work and apply targeted skills and strategies with teacher support.
Teacher controls the learning	Student controls the learning

Figure 1:2 A comparison of guided reading and supported independent reading.

The First Essential of Supported Independent Reading: Self-Selected Texts

Almost 10 years ago, the literacy team at the intermediate school where I was content specialist decided to turn the classrooms there into true reading workshops. All of us believed this approach would be the most beneficial for our students, many of whom lived lives away from school that allowed no time for reading and afforded no good place to curl up with a good book.

We weren't 2 weeks into the school year before teachers started throwing their hands in the air and wailing, "These kids don't know how to choose books. We go to the library, they walk around for 10 minutes or play on the card catalog, then just grab books off the shelves and check them out. How can I get a reading workshop going if the kids can't read the books they've got?" We even had kids who spoke absolutely no Spanish checking out Spanish books. That is how much effort they were putting into book selection.

Daniels and Bizar (2005) list student choice as one of the important characteristics of "best practice" classrooms, and student choice has continually been shown to increase intrinsic motivation in learners (Guthrie & Knowles, 2001). Even reluctant readers can have positive attitudes toward reading that they themselves have chosen (Worthy, 1996). It is imperative that students be empowered to choose their own texts—and to read them with a sense of joy.

Because reluctant readers are just that—reluctant—it is easier to place a book in their hands and require its reading than it is to teach them to find the books on their own. Well-meaning teachers put these students in guided reading groups where the *teacher* has chosen the book; they may even put them in literature study groups where the *teacher* has either directly chosen the book or narrowed the choice to three or four titles deemed to be appropriate, usually based on reading level. These teachers might argue that they *do* let students choose their own books in the library—but the students are reading these all on their own and they are not being held accountable for the reading. So, these books often go into tote trays, backpacks, or lockers for 2 weeks and are then turned in to be replaced by other books that will meet the same fate.

Several years ago, at their teacher's request, I escorted a group of five totally disengaged readers to the library, hoping to help them find a book they might enjoy. We sat down at a round table in the library to talk about how readers choose books. Their body language spoke volumes—they slumped in their chairs, arms crossed across their chests, heads thrown back. Heavy sighs filled the air.

"Tell me what kinds of books you like," I began.

"I don't like books," one particularly surly young man volunteered.

"Not even the books your teacher reads aloud to you?" I asked.

"Nope—I told you. I don't like *any* books," he continued.

"But your teacher requires you to read 30 minutes every day, doesn't she?"

"Yep."

"So what do you do?"

"Turn the pages and pretend."

"Do you check books out of the library?"

"Yep—our teacher makes us."

"Then what?"

"I put them in my desk and leave them there until we come back to the library. Then I turn them in."

"What do you read during class?"

"I just pull something off the teacher's shelf. I told you—I don't really *read* it—I just pretend."

"Have you ever read a book all the way through?"

"Are you kidding me?"

To avoid this type of disengagement, teachers must make clear to students that their job in the library is to choose books they intend to read all the way through. If students are never actually expected to finish the books they choose, is it any wonder that they develop such cavalier attitudes toward reading?

If students are going to be given 30 minutes a day to read, they need to make good book choices. However, students must be *taught* to do so. This teaching starts with the teacher's explanation of how readers choose books to read.

When dedicated readers choose a book to read, they always look for a book they think they will enjoy. Their initial interest in the book they choose is usually piqued either by something they learned in school, by seeing authors interviewed on television, by talking to other readers, or by having a personal need to know. Students need to be told that people use these experiences to drive their book selections. They need to be told that readers actually intend to find interesting books and to finish them.

Since students' expectations for their reading are key to their motivation to read (McKenna, 2001), it is essential that teachers explicitly teach an expectation of joy. No readers finish books they aren't enjoying if they have a choice. Since students are still learning to find the kinds of books they will like and many need expert guidance in this skill, it is important for the teacher to learn about each student's interests.

This can be accomplished with an assignment such as Fascinating You (Appendix A), an activity that can prove invaluable in helping guide students to books. Students' answers to questions about their family and where they have lived can be used to help steer them toward realistic fiction books whose characters have families or problems much like their own or toward books set in places that are familiar to them. Their answers about their out-of-school activities can help determine which nonfiction books to showcase so that they can discover that there are nonfiction books about the sports they like, biographies of the singers they listen to, and even sports fiction revolving around the sports they themselves play.

Teachers should write answers to the same questions their students will answer. As they share their own interests, teachers should explicitly teach students how they use their life experiences and interests to choose books, stressing always that this starts with an intention to enjoy the reading experience. Real readers always expect to *finish* and *enjoy* the books they read—students must be taught to expect nothing less.

The Second Essential of Supported Independent Reading: Choosing to Grow

A commitment to student choice must be coupled with a commitment to teaching students to choose texts that will further their growth as readers. Carver's (2000) research shows that students who read books that interest them but that are not sufficiently difficult do not show increased levels of reading achievement. It is a teacher's responsibility to guide students to books at appropriate levels of challenge.

This is not always an easy thing to do. Many intermediate students who have continual struggles with reading are very reluctant to leave the comfort of picture books and move into chapter books. Although more and more picture books are being written at higher reading levels, reading only in texts that can be finished in one sitting does not build the type of stamina needed to tackle more advanced texts. These books also do not help students learn to carry information across from one chapter to the next or to sustain their interest in the problem and its solution. It would be easier to continue to supply picture books to these students—their reading of these books would require very little intervention—but would the time these students spent on these short texts help accelerate their growth as readers?

Older students sometimes cling to the familiarity of series books rather than making the transition to more sophisticated texts with characters who are older and whose problems more closely mirror their own. Without support from a skilled reader who can guide them through their first experience with these more complicated texts, these readers may not make the transition to age-appropriate reading. If students are to grow as readers, they must be reading texts at increasingly higher levels of difficulty.

Supported independent reading should be done in texts at levels that produce what Caine and Caine (1994) call "relaxed alertness," that is, levels that provide enough challenge to be interesting but enough familiarity to be manageable. Students who continually read at a level that presents no challenges for them will make no more gains than students who spend the same amount of time doing activities other than reading (Carver, 2000). If students are to thrive as readers, they cannot afford 30 minutes each day of wasted time.

It is essential that students know what their reading level actually is. This is a tricky line to walk—because very below-level students can feel humiliated and defeated before they ever pick up a book if quality teaching does not precede these revelations. It is important that teachers help students understand that if they are reading below level, it is an indication that they have not read enough—*not* that they are not as smart as the on-level readers around them. They can catch up if they read, read, and read some more in books that they actually enjoy and understand.

Students need to understand that reading books that are too difficult for them does not make them better readers—it just makes them hate reading. They become so frustrated by the work they are having to do just to get through a page of text and so confused by things that are well above what Vygotsky (1978) calls their actual development that they just give up and decide the problem is that they hate reading—not that they are in the wrong text.

I was once required to read Vygotsky's (1986) book, *Thought and Language*. To say that book was above my actual level of development would be a mild understatement. I am a fast reader—but I would agonizingly make my way through that text, dictionary at my side. Sometimes it would take me 15–20 minutes to read one page.

What if that were my experience with *every* book I read? What if every single text I held were at that same level of difficulty? *Why* would I ever want to read anything?

Some of our students are in just that predicament—*everything* they are required to read in school is above their level of actual development. If they do not learn to choose books to read for enjoyment that are at a level that requires much less attention to the work of decoding and determining the meaning of new words and if they are not given time during the school day to read these books, they may never develop into the type of person who loves books and reading.

It is still essential that students understand that finding a book that *interests* them should come *before* checking its reading level. Students can read slightly above their level if they have a wealth of prior knowledge about the subject of the book. This is especially true in nonfiction texts, which are often the text of choice for reluctant readers as well as many middle school students (Jobe & Dayton-Sakari, 1999; Carter & Abrahamson, 1998; Lesesne, 2006).

Because readers must be able to choose books anywhere, students must be taught to choose books at an appropriate reading level for them. The best strategy I have ever found for helping students learn to make this important choice is the five-finger rule.

The five-finger rule is really quite simple. Readers open books under consideration to a page somewhere in the middle of the book and skim down the page looking for words they don't know. Every time they find an unfamiliar word, they hold up one finger. If they have five fingers up at the bottom of the page, the book is too difficult. If they have no fingers up at all, the book is probably too easy and will not spur the desired growth.

Students should do this on two or three pages before deciding whether the book is at the right level for them to read. One page may not give a true picture of the book's level. Students also need to understand the meaning of the word *skim*. This strategy is a quick assessment—it shouldn't take a lot of time. If students are trying to actually *read* a text that is going to prove to be too hard, it will slow them down.

Students should be given opportunities to practice this strategy before ever going to the library. They should sit in groups with stacks of books in front of them at all sorts of reading levels and use the five-finger rule to assess whether or not the book would be right for them. On a sheet of paper, they should write down the titles and authors of each book and rate each one as either too easy, too hard, or just right. That is why many elementary teachers call the five-finger rule the Goldilocks rule—students are trying out different texts, looking for something that is "just right." By walking around the room as the students practice, teachers can be sure each student understands how to use this helpful strategy. By reviewing their lists and ratings later, teachers can get a clearer view of each student's reading level.

Setting the Stage for Finding Books in the Library

It is essential to have a deep discussion not only of how readers choose books, but also of how they find them in a library. Some students have never been to a public library; many have never been deeply taught how to find a book in one; most have never been asked to go to the library and find a book they expect to finish and enjoy. The choices students make on the very first library day will determine how quickly supported independent reading begins to spur student growth.

It is one thing for students to know what kind of book they want to find—and quite another to actually locate it in the vast wasteland of bookshelves that is alien territory to far too many of our students.

The discussion can start with a simple question: "How do you find a book you want to read in the library?" Anticipating what they think their teacher wants to hear, students will undoubtedly suggest going to the card catalog. This question should be followed up with the question, "Who can explain to me how to use the card catalog?" After a great deal of wait time, this question is usually answered in a very general way: "You type in the kind of book you want and it tells you where to find it."

All follow-up questions should be directed not to the student who offered the suggestion, but to the class as a whole, always beginning with, "Who can tell me. . . .?" By immediately quizzing students who are brave enough to answer the initial question, students are liable to fear that their ideas are being devalued. There is no faster way to shut down student thinking than to appear skeptical about the validity of their suggestions.

Initial answers that address physical actions, such as typing in the card catalog or pulling a book from the shelf, should be followed up with questions that cause the students to explain the *thinking* that occurs before the action (Fig. 1:3). Often, this will lead to a teachable moment, where the teacher can offer expert guidance just at the point of need. In the case of the card catalog, this is a chance to explicitly teach that the card catalog can be sorted three ways—by title, by subject, or by author. Readers who plan to finish and enjoy the books they choose have a purpose when they go to the card catalog—they are going to find another book written by an author they enjoy, a specific book they've heard about from another reader, or a book in a genre or about a topic in which they already know they are interested. Sitting in front of a computerized card catalog is not a technology exercise—it is a step in finding the next best book they've ever read.

By asking the right questions, the teacher is supporting the thinking of students who are just beginning to learn that choice is always coupled with responsibility. Yes, they will be allowed to choose their own books to read, as long as they show that they are responsible enough to choose wisely. If their choices are *not* wise, the teacher will offer guidance until they show that they are, in fact, capable of choosing responsibly.

Student Suggestion	Follow-Up Question	On-the-Spot Minilesson
I just go find the one I want.	Who can tell me how to decide what kind of book I want?	Readers use what they already know to help them find books to read; they look for authors they like, series they enjoy, books other people have recommended, or books about subjects they're interested in.
I go to the shelves and find one I like.	Who can tell me how you know which shelf to go to in the library?	The library has three sections: the fiction section, the nonfiction section, and the reference section.
I go to the card catalog.	Who can tell me how to use the card catalog?	Card catalogs are library tools that help us find the books we are looking for.
I type in the kind of book I want.	Who can tell me how to decide what to type in the search area of the card catalog?	Card catalogs can be sorted by author, title, or subject. Readers think about these things when choosing a book.
I ask the librarian to help me find a good book.	Who can tell me what kind of question they might ask the librarian?	Readers ask librarians for specific help by already knowing what kind of book they might want and asking for suggestions or help in finding it in the library.
I just start looking at the books until I find one I like.	Who can tell me what to do when I'm standing in front of a bookshelf so that I can find a book I like?	Readers preview books by looking at the cover and reading the summaries on the back or on the front flyleaf.

Figure 1:3 Sample follow-up questions and minilessons to support student choice: How do you choose a book in the library?

Preparing for the Unexpected

Teachers cannot make assumptions about what experiences their students have had or what their students are able to do. Unless teachers enjoy living on the edge or dealing with frustration, students should *never* be taken to the library until the teacher has invested time teaching them how to make good choices once they get there. Teachers should be sure that the answers to all of the following questions are *yes* before the students ever line them up at the classroom door:

- Do your students understand that they should choose a book they expect to finish and enjoy?
- Do your students know that there are two sections in the library—fiction and nonfiction—and how to find a book in each one?
- Have you spent time showcasing both fiction and nonfiction books that may interest your students?
- Have you given your students time to talk to each other about books they have read and enjoyed?
- Do your students know what a card catalog is and how to use it?
- Do your students understand what the information on the spines of library books tells us?
- Do your students know how to preview a book to see if they will like it?
- Do your students know their reading levels and how to find books at the proper reading level for growth?
- Have your students *practiced* the five-finger-rule method of judging a book's readability?
- Do your students know exactly what kind of book they are looking for before they ever leave your classroom?

Dealing with Poor Choices

No matter how much time is spent teaching students to make good choices, some will still choose poorly. They are either not yet committed to finding books they will enjoy, or they still don't understand how to do that. These poor choices cannot be ignored—they must be addressed.

Library time for students is not free time for teachers. This is not the time for teachers to run to the restroom, make a quick phone call, or chat with the librarian; this is the time to offer guidance when it is needed most—while students are actually trying to choose the books they will enjoy and finish.

Likewise, library time is not social hour for students. Before ever leaving the classroom, expectations must be made clear—students will be actively looking for books to read and will speak only to adults who can help them locate titles they might enjoy. It is also helpful to have students write three ideas for books on slips of paper before they ever leave the classroom, so that the teacher can see that they are putting thought into their choices. This also gives them a chance to ask their classmates the titles or authors of books they might like to read so that these conversations aren't necessary once they get to the library. One of the best teachers I know stands by the check-out counter in the library and personally inspects every book students are planning to check out. If they have not made good reading choices, she accompanies them back to the shelves to choose again.

I believe students should always read in self-selected texts during supported independent reading time. However, for students who are overwhelmed by the amount of books available to them, I often offer five or six suggestions. I actually put the book choices in the students' hands, if at all possible. If they still have trouble choosing, I might narrow the choices even further or ask them to tell me what they'd like to have in a book that none of my choices has offered—and then I get some more choices for them to preview. I try *never* to choose a book for a student—but I occasionally break even that rule if I think it is in the student's best interest. However, I try every trick I know to get them into books more or less on their own before I step in and choose for them—and in a normal school year, I can count on one hand the number of books I have chosen for students and asked them to read.

The Third Essential: Teacher Monitoring and Intervention

Supported independent reading, again, is reading done in mostly self-selected texts written at appropriate levels to spur growth in which the actual reading of the texts is *monitored by a teacher who intervenes, as necessary, to insure success.* This monitoring is the necessary component for success.

Think back to the time when you drove with a learner's permit. Those were the days when another driver with a license had to be sitting in the passenger seat every time you drove. The first experienced driver who watched you learn was probably your driver's education instructor, who could slam on a brake discretely hidden on his side of the car to keep you from backing into a ditch.

Think of independent reading time as time spent in the passenger seat watching someone else learn to love reading. As the instructor, you have already proven to the powers that be that *you* know how to do this, and you are giving the students with whom you work the freedom to try on their own, but you have that magic brake that can stop them when they are about to crash and burn.

It is essential that teachers monitor students during independent reading time. Left to their own devices, many of the readers in the room will choose other activities to fill their time, activities they have already learned to enjoy, such as sleeping, daydreaming, writing notes, or bothering their friends. There are not enough truly engaged readers in the typical classroom to make independent reading time productive without this essential supervision. It is the teacher's responsibility to lead every student in the room to success and joy in reading. It is a responsibility that must be taken seriously—lifetime readers are at stake.

References

Caine, R. N., & Caine, G. (1994). *Making connections: Teaching and the human brain.* Menlo Park, CA: Addison-Wesley.

Calkins, L. M. (2001). *The art of teaching reading.* New York: Addison-Wesley.

Carter, B., & Abrahamson, R. F. (1998). Castles to Colin Powell: The truth about nonfiction. In K. Beers & B. G. Samuels (Eds.), *Into focus: Understanding and creating middle school readers* (pp. 313–331). Norwood, MA: Christopher-Gordon.

Carver, R. P. (2000). *The causes of high and low reading achievement.* Mahwah, NJ: Lawrence Erlbaum.

Daniels, H., & Bizar, M. (2005). *Teaching the best practice way: Methods that matter, K–12.* Portland, ME: Stenhouse.

Fountas, I. C., & Pinnell, G. S. (2001). *Guiding readers and writers grades 3–6.* Portsmouth, NH: Heinemann.

Gallagher, M., & Pearson, P. D. (1983). *The instruction of reading comprehension. Contemporary Educational Psychology, 8,* 317–344.

Guthrie, J. T., & Knowles, K. T. (2001). Promoting reading motivation. In L. Verhoeven & C. Snow (Eds.), *Literacy and motivation: Reading engagement in individuals and groups* (pp. 159–176). Mahwah, NJ: Lawrence Erlbaum.

jobe, R., & Dayton-Sakari, M. (1999). *Reluctant readers.* Markham, Ontario, Canada: Pembroke.

Lesesne, T. S. (2006). *Naked reading: Uncovering what tweens need to become lifelong readers.* Portland, ME: Stenhouse.

McKenna, M. C. (2001). Development of reading attitudes. In L. Verhoeven & C. Snow (Eds.), *Literacy and motivation: Reading engagement in individuals and groups* (pp. 135–158). Mahwah, NJ: Lawrence Erlbaum.

Vygotsky, L. S. (1978). *Mind in society: The development of higher psychological processes.* Cambridge, MA: Harvard University Press.

Vygotsky, L. S. (1986). *Thought and language.* Cambridge, MA: MIT Press.

Worthy, J. (1996). Removing barriers to voluntary reading: The role of school and classroom libraries. *Language Arts, 73,* 484–492.

Trade Books Cited

Jacques, B. (1988). *Mossflower*. New York: Philomel Books.

Paolini, C. (2005). *Eldest*. New York: Alfred A. Knopf.

Chapter 2

Providing Structures for Growth

It was the third week of the semester for the graduate students enrolled in the Critical Components of Intermediate Balanced Literacy course I was teaching. We had done the get-acquainted session and had an overview of balanced literacy. Now it was time to get down to business; we were starting the first of two 3-hour sessions on independent reading. I had already explained the importance of time for independent reading during the school day and was launching into the reasons why independent reading should be the first critical component to be put into place when a very skilled teacher near the middle of the room raised her hand.

"But I can't possibly spend all this time on independent reading," she said. "I have to be doing guided reading groups *every single day*."

"Okay," I nodded. "But what exactly are the kids who aren't with you doing?"

"They're reading."

I completely understood this teacher's view of the importance of guided reading; it is a view I share, and we would spend several 3-hour sessions on it—including how to structure learning centers to engage students in meaningful activities while the teacher pulls a small group. Like so many other teachers I know, this wonderful professional did not realize the impact *supported* independent reading could have on her students as skilled readers in training. She saw independent reading as an activity that would keep the students busy while she guided struggling readers to success. From the first week of school, the

baskets of books they could choose to read
like the sustained silent reading model, the
ole for their reading; they were just expected

Structure of Supported Independent Reading

In contrast to independent reading designed as an activity to keep students busy, supported independent reading should have a definite structure. Since brain research shows predictability reduces stress (Jensen, 1998), this important instructional time follows a predictable pattern:

- minilesson to review prior learning
- note-taking assignment
- logging in
- student reading and teacher conferencing
- logging out
- completing the notes

If carefully planned and effectively carried out, supported independent reading will consume 45–60 minutes a day.

My former district provided 90-minute reading blocks at both the intermediate and middle school levels, a luxury of time for which teachers were grateful. But I have taught in a middle school classroom with 45-minute class periods and currently work in a middle school with classes that are 65 minutes long, so I have experienced these time restraints as well. Supported independent reading can be used successfully in any configuration.

With only 45 minutes a day and responsibility for teaching both reading and writing, I could not do supported independent reading every day. Likewise, teachers who only have 60 minutes a day for reading may have to alternate days of supported independent reading with days of learning centers and guided reading or direct instruction. The important goal, no matter how much time is available, is to make every second count.

Teacher Responsibilities

For supported independent reading to be effective, the teacher must fulfill these responsibilities:

- provide the materials necessary for student success and accountability—a room full of books at various levels and in various genres, reading logs and folders, comfortable places to sit (or lie down) and read, a clipboard and forms or paper on which to take anecdotal notes
- explicitly teach expectations for student behavior—and enforce those expectations every single day with every single student
- plan short, focused minilessons to review and reinforce student understanding of the skills and strategies competent readers employ
- plan daily note-taking assignments that will assess student understanding of the minilesson and its application to real reading *without* interrupting the flow of the reading
- approach each day with a genuine curiosity about what stands in the way for each individual reader's success—and a sincere desire to remove that roadblock
- spend every second of supported independent reading time every day conferencing with students at their desks or wherever they have chosen to read
- establish an efficient system for taking daily notes on student behaviors and progress
- experiment with different responses to problems, discarding ones that don't seem to work and reusing those that lead to success
- teach reading—not test taking—during this critical instructional time
- above all, determine that *every* student in the room will find success and joy in reading—and show that determination in every word said and every decision made every day

The Classroom Library

One of the keys to motivating students to read is to create a classroom culture centered on reading (McKenna, 2001). The pivotal element in this climate is the classroom library. This library should be stocked with both narrative and informational texts at all levels—on level, below level, and above level—to address the varying needs of the readers in the classroom.

Research continually shows that access to books positively impacts reading achievement (Allington, 2001; Krashen, 2004). The more books, the better—Routman (2000) suggests a minimum of at least five to six books per student, while Allington (2001) recommends having 500 titles available!

The intermediate school in which I worked had a literacy center that housed literally hundreds of books in all genres and at all levels. This center was a valuable resource for the reading teachers in the building. The books there were arranged by genre and by approximate reading level within each genre. The collection included nonfiction as well as fiction, current titles as well as classics. Every effort had been made to find books that reflected all the varying cultures whose children walked through the doors of the school each day. There were no class sets of single titles because even the all-gifted classrooms had readers at varying levels, and a single text would not fit every reader in the room.

As teachers worked with students, they got a sense of what interested them, went to the center, and pulled stacks of books to use in book groups or to place strategically in the classroom. They simply placed these books in a prominent position and said, "I brought some books I thought you might like with me today. I'll leave them right here—when you get a chance, feel free to look at them. Remember that you have to have a book on your desk ready to read before we start independent reading today." Other teachers in the building rotated books from the center in and out of their classroom libraries to keep the titles fresh.

The middle school where I taught did not have these resources available, so I stocked my classroom library myself. I paid attention to the books the kids were reading and made sure I got those into my classroom—either through book club orders, half-price book stores, and the regular chain booksellers.

Teachers, however, are not famous for their unlimited bank accounts. Particularly for teachers who are new to the profession and have not yet built up an extensive library collection, it is important to look for cost-effective ways to build their libraries. Half-price and used bookstores, garage sales, and library book sales can stretch dollars, as can the various mail-order book clubs. By previewing book club fliers and briefly talking about the books listed there, teachers can greatly increase the number of books the students buy. This earns the teacher bonus points, and those bonus points add up. It is possible for a teacher to add hundreds of titles to the library in a year by spending book club bonus points.

There are other ways to build the collection that cost the teacher absolutely no money at all. One creative way to fill the shelves is to encourage students to bring in books they have at home that they are finished reading. Some teachers do this mid-year and allow students to trade the books they bring for another book from the library. This gives the library a fresh, new look. Other teachers give rewards, such as free homework passes, extra computer time, lunch with the teacher, or extra in-class reading time for bringing in books. Classroom book drives often result in parents donating titles to the class. Public libraries are another good resource, as they will usually check out stacks of books to teachers for up to 6 weeks. School librarians will often put together a cart of books that can be taken to the classroom for student checkout. No matter how it is done, filling the classroom with as many books as possible should be an essential goal of every reading teacher.

Teachers should talk regularly with their librarians about the books that are popular with the kids, especially since adults don't always enjoy the genres currently popular with students. Books listed as Children's Choices or Young Adult Choices by the International Reading Association each year and those that win state book awards are always good choices. By actively looking for books students will enjoy, teachers take an important step toward filling classrooms not only with books, but also with eager readers.

Teachers arrange their classroom libraries in a host of different ways. Some just place them on shelves in no particular order; some put them in baskets or sections by genre. I personally like to arrange books by genre, so that students can look for the type of book they already know they like.

Although Calkins (2001) makes a convincing argument for leveled libraries, I am still committed to the idea of teaching students to make correct choices without leveling, particularly in the intermediate- and middle school grades. Bookstores and libraries don't put dots on book spines and direct readers to the correct colored dot. This commitment to student choice requires vigilance on the part of the teacher, who must know both the readers and the texts and must be willing to intervene when poor choices are made, but it more closely replicates reading in the world outside of school.

When teachers ask for advice on stocking their classroom libraries, I always recommend starting with authors who have written a number of books that seem to appeal to the students (Figs. 2:1–2:3). If students enjoy the first book by that author, they can use that knowledge to help them choose another book by the same author. Authors such as Lois Lowry, Paula Danziger, and Louis Sachar write books at varying levels and even in various genres, so they are important to include in the classroom library. Finding an author they love is an important first step toward building students' lifetime love of reading.

Avi	C.S. Lewis
Lynne Reid Banks	Lois Lowry
Judy Blume	D. J. MacHale
Clyde Robert Bulla	Patricia MacLachlan
Eve Bunting	Stephen Manes
Betsy Byars	Ann M. Martin
Meg Cabot	Megan McDonald
Matt Christopher	Phyllis Reynolds Naylor
Beverly Cleary	Jenny Nimmo
Andrew Clements	Garth Nix
Eoin Colfer	Joan Lowery Nixon
Ellen Conford	Scott O'Dell
Caroline B. Cooney	Mary Pope Osborne
Bruce Coville	Christopher Paolini
Sharon Creech	Barbara Park
Christopher Paul Curtis	Katherine Paterson
Roald Dahl	Gary Paulsen
Paula Danziger	Richard Peck
Barthe DeClements	Rodman Philbrick
Carl Deuker	Dav Pilkey
Kate DiCamillo	J.K. Rowling
Lois Duncan	Willo Davis Roberts
Nancy Farmer	Thomas Rockwell
John D. Fitzgerald	Pam Munoz Ryan
Sid Fleischman	Cynthia Rylant
Cornelia Funke	Louis Sachar
Patricia Reilly Giff	Neil Schusterman
Jack Gantos	William Sleator
Jean Craighead George	Lemony Snicket
Jamie Gilson	Zilpha Keatley Snyder
Dan Gutman	Donald Sobol
Margaret Peterson Haddix	Gary Soto
Mary Downing Hahn	Jerry Spinelli
Virginia Hamilton	R.L. Stine
Karen Hesse	Mildred D. Taylor
Dan Hiaasen	Theodore Taylor
Will Hobbs	J.R.R. Tolkien
James Howe	Wendelin Van Draanen
Joanna Hurwitz	Bill Wallace
Brian Jacques	Gertrude Chandler Warner
Peg Kehret	E. B. White
E.L. Konigsberg	Elizabeth Winthrop
Gordon Korman	Betty Ren Wright
Gail Carson Levine	Laurence Yep

Figure 2:1 Never-fail authors for intermediate classroom libraries: fiction.

Laurie Halse Anderson	Jamie Gilson	Scott O'Dell
Amelia Atwater-Rhodes	Linda Glovach	Christopher Paolini
Mary Jane Auch	Nikki Grimes	Barbara Park
Avi	Dan Gutman	Katherine Paterson
T. A. Barron	Margaret Peterson Haddix	Gary Paulsen
Joan Bauer	Mary Downing Hahn	Richard Peck
Judy Blume	Virginia Hamilton	Rodman Philbrick
Eve Bunting	Karen Hesse	Celia Rees
Betsy Byars	Dan Hiaasen	Ann Rinaldi
Meg Cabot	Will Hobbs	J.K. Rowling
Matt Christopher	Anthony Horowitz	Willo Davis Roberts
Beverly Cleary	James Howe	Pam Munoz Ryan
Andrew Clements	Joanna Hurwitz	Cynthia Rylant
Eoin Colfer	Brian Jacques	Louis Sachar
Caroline B. Cooney	Peg Kehret	Neil Schusterman
Robert Cormier	David Klass	William Sleator
Bruce Coville	E.L. Konigsberg	Roland Smith
Sharon Creech	Gordon Korman	Lemony Snicket
Marianne Curley	Kathryn Lasky	Zilpha Keatley Snyder
Christopher Paul Curtis	Gail Carson Levine	Donald Sobol
Roald Dahl	C.S. Lewis	Gary Soto
Paula Danziger	Lois Lowry	Jerry Spinelli
Barthe DeClements	Patricia MacLachlan	R.L. Stine
Sarah Dessen	Carolyn Mackler	Todd Strasser
Carl Deuker	Stephen Manes	Mildred D. Taylor
Kate DiCamillo	Ann M. Martin	Theodore Taylor
Sharon M. Draper	Norma Fox Mazer	J.R.R. Tolkien
Lois Duncan	Megan McDonald	Wendelin Van Draanen
Nancy Farmer	D. J. MacHale	Cynthia Voigt
Jean Ferris	Carolyn Meyer	Bill Wallace
Sharon Flake	Ben Mikaelson	E. B. White
Sid Fleischman	Walter Dean Myers	Elizabeth Winthrop
Alex Flinn	Phyllis Reynolds Naylor	Jacqueline Woodson
Cornelia Funke	Jenny Nimmo	Laurence Yep
Jack Gantos	Garth Nix	Paul Zindel
Jean Craighead George	Joan Lowery Nixon	

Figure 2:2 Never-fail authors for middle school classroom libraries: fiction.

Robert D. Ballard Jon Finkel Russell Freedman Robert Genat Gail Gibbons Michael Green Wilborn Hampton Chris Hayhurst Cathy Hopkins Mark Huebner Kathleen Krull Gregory Leland Joel Levy Julius Lester David MacCauley	Joy Masoff Jim Murphy Walter Dean Myers John Nichols Gary Paulsen Andrea Davis Pinkney Laurence Pringle David West Reynolds Tucker Shaw Terry Sievert Seymour Simon Diane Stanley Shelley Tanaka Jane Yolen

Figure 2:3 Never-fail authors for classroom libraries: nonfiction.

The classroom library should be a stress-free environment. Students should feel comfortable pulling books from the shelves, previewing them, and taking them to their desks and homes. The books should be there for the students, not for the teacher.

I believe that classroom library books are there to be read. And sometimes—no matter how vigilant the teacher might be—books disappear. I quit using a check-out system for my books years ago. If a book disappears from my shelf because it went home with a student who wanted to read it, that—to me—is not only an occupational hazard, but a tribute to the fact that I am giving students access to the books they truly want to read.

Do I lose some books every year? Of course I do. Even libraries with detector systems lose books. I am continually putting new titles on the shelves, so the few that are missing are regularly replaced. I write my name in black marker on the edge of the leaves on the righthand side, so if the books are found in the hallway or in lockers, it's easy to return them to me.

The students know I have put these books there for them. I think of them as the *students'* books and teach them to feel the same way. If they don't return a book they've borrowed, they have hurt the other students more than they have hurt me. Because my commitment is to creating an environment that nurtures readers, I consider losing books a tribute to the time I have spent helping students learn to love reading. I don't expect every teacher to adopt this way of thinking—but it has made my classroom library a stress-free environment for me as well as for my students.

Reading

Because supported independent reading tin[...]
need to be held accountable for the way this t[...]
log in the book they are reading each day on a [...]

While the students consider this only a way of [...]
doing, their reading logs are invaluable assessment[...]
ing their logs, teachers can identify uncommitted [...] ...ge books
every day and begin to work with these students o[...] .g better choices.
They can look at how many pages are being read each day and identify students who are making very slow progress and may be in books that are too hard for them. By looking at the pages where they start and end each day, teachers can see which students are actually reading their books at home, no matter what they may put on their at-home reading assignment. Reading logs tell teachers which students love fantasy and which prefer realistic fiction. They tell who has read just about every book in a series and will need help moving into other books. And reading logs tell far more about a student's reading level than any one-time assessment ever will.

In my middle school classroom, the students dedicated the first ten pages or so of a spiral notebook to their reading log. The students created columns for the date, the book's author and title, the page on which they started, and the page on which they ended (Fig. 2:4). The rest of the notebook was filled with their reading responses.

Date	Title and Author	Page Started	Page Finished
9/04	*Walk Two Moons* by Sharon Creech	3	15
9/05	Same	20	35
9/06	Same	55	75

Figure 2:4 A sample reading log.

Because some teachers want to generate a daily grade each week for the pages read during independent reading, a daily reading log can be useful (Appendix B). Students who are reading a book at the correct level should be able to read at least 10 pages in 30 minutes, so that is the number on which a grade could be based. Students would be expected to read 50 pages a week, each page being worth two points. A student who read only 30 pages that week would receive a 60 for a daily grade. If the logs are copied on both sides of a page, one sheet of paper is good for 2 weeks. This same information can also be generated

...nts in their reading notebooks rather than on separate sheets of paper. ...hese logs should be kept in student reading folders that are readily available for parent conferences. It is important to have a place for these logs so that students can find them quickly. Since much of what leaves the classroom never finds its way back, it is a good idea to require these logs to be left in the classroom. If the room is in rows, students can pass their folders or notebooks to the front where the teacher can collect them; if the students are in groups, the folders or notebooks can be stacked in the center of the group and picked up there. If the logs and notebooks are lost, valuable assessment information disappears, so it is important to take extremely good care of these treasures.

Teaching Expectations

I have a love/hate relationship with the beginning of the school year. I love the look of new folders, new notebooks, new pens and pencils. My markers all work, my shelves are all straight, and the borderette around all my bulletin boards is all neatly stapled. Books I discovered over the summer are waiting for students to read—and there are dozens of new young people for me to get to know. I truly can't wait. That's the love part.

The hate part is that I am used to having students who come in every day and know exactly what to do—and now I am starting from scratch and have to teach the new residents of my classroom exactly how this neighborhood of ours works. I'd rather just teach reading—but I know that teaching these expectations is vitally important to every student's success.

The expectations for supported independent reading time are simple:

- Have a book on your desk ready to read when reading time begins.
- Log in on your reading log before you begin reading.
- Read for the entire 30 minutes.
- Log out on your reading log and complete your response assignment.

These expectations should be posted at the front of the room—but they must also be taught.

When I work with new teachers as they learn to set up their classrooms and write their lesson plans, my advice is always this: Picture what would happen if everything went wrong—and teach to avoid that chaos. Veteran teachers all agree that time spent teaching expectations and routines is time well spent. The first expectation for independent reading time that must be taught is that the books the students read will be at their desks *before* independent reading time arrives.

Chaos will ensue if students do not have books to read during independent reading time. Students can find countless ways to waste an entire 30 minutes finding a book to read. They give all kinds of reasons for why they don't have one—they left the book at home, they left it in their locker, they lost it, they finished it, they didn't like it. But whatever the reason, they don't have anything to read—so reading time will be totally wasted.

The first order of business should be introducing students to the classroom library and teaching them how it works. Students should know from the beginning that these books are not decorations—they are sweet temptations meant to whet their appetites for reading. They should be encouraged to look at these books at every appropriate time. Appropriate times include when they first arrive in the classroom, when they have finished their classwork and asked permission to visit the library, before or after school with teacher permission and a pass. Students should *not* be crowded around the shelves during independent reading time. Time spent at the shelves is time that is *not* spent reading.

Students know when they are nearing the end of a book—and should be taught that readers already know what they are going to read next. They should have the next book picked out and at their desk before they ever read that final word. Students also know when they have forgotten their book at home, and they should be expected to choose a new book from the library before reading time begins.

If we want our students to be readers, we have to teach them to think like readers. Readers never go anywhere without a book. They have two or three in a bag for long airplane trips in case they finish one of them. They have books on their desks at work, books at home, and books in the car. They want to be able to read every chance they get—and teachers should want their students to learn these same habits.

In intermediate classrooms, students can keep books in their desks or tote trays ready to read. In middle school classrooms, students can tag books with sticky notes and leave them on a table or the teacher's desk so that if they arrive without a book, one would be available when reading time begins. If the teacher requires that every student has a book ready to read at the beginning of independent reading time and enforces that expectation, it will become a habit for students.

Early in the year, I keep a stack of books on my desk—fiction and nonfiction books at various reading levels. If a student does not have a book to read, I choose three or four books from the stack, place them on the student's desk, and expect one to be chosen for reading. As I get to know my students better, I can predict which students won't have books—and I will be ready, armed before they arrive with several titles I have chosen just for them that are at the right reading level and should be of interest. I will allow them to choose the one they will read—but it will *not* involve standing at the shelves in the classroom library.

Students need to know that their teacher expects them to read for the entire 30 minutes. Reading does not mean writing or talking or staring into space—reading means reading. Early in the year, a lot of conferencing time will be spent redirecting disengaged readers—but the teacher's persistence will pay off. In time, the students will believe that they are expected to spend independent reading time actually reading.

The Minilesson

Skilled readers know that they always read for a purpose. They read newspapers to find out what is going on in their communities and in the world. They read magazines to learn about people, places, and issues that interest them. They read some books just to get lost in characters and imaginary situations, others to help them learn more about their profession or about the world. Many students read because a teacher or parent told them to—period.

Minilessons are a chance to remind students *how* and *why* people read. They are an opportunity to make clear to students that reading is not moving our eyes across a string of letters. Reading is thinking about the words on the page.

There is a reason for the prefix *mini* in this context. *Mini*, of course, means small—and a *mini*lesson should be just that. These quick reminders before reading should be short, sweet, and to the point. If their purpose is only to address procedural issues, they can introduce new information, such as how to fill out a reading log or how to request a conference. But 15 minutes or less is not enough time to *teach* skills, such as inferencing, or strategies, such as visualizing; it is enough time to *review* these skills, but not to introduce them. These lessons should be *taught* in-depth and for understanding in a block of time separate from that set aside for independent reading. *Mini*, after all, suggests that there is a larger version of this lesson somewhere.

Teachers are about to ask students to try to do something independently—and this comes near the end of the gradual release model of instruction (Gallagher & Pearson, 1983). All the other elements of the model, such as teacher modeling through think alouds and guided practice in groups or with partners, should already have occurred before students are expected to try the skill or strategy alone.

Providing Structures for Growth

When teachers try to take students all the way through model in one day, they are expecting far too much. To strategy, model it through a think aloud, have students pr situation, and then ask them to do it independently is asking person in a day. Brain research has shown that students need what they have learned (Jensen, 1998). If we give them too much ination at one time, we have diminished their chances to actually learn it. We should stretch the learning—and the gradual release model—out over a period of time, stopping along the way to reteach, if necessary. By the time we are ready for the students to practice the skill alone, a quick review should be enough to get them on their way.

Unless it is a procedural minilesson whose purpose is just to teach classroom expectations, the minilesson before independent reading has three purposes:

- to remind students of a skill or strategy that will help them read with deeper understanding
- to set a purpose for the day's reading
- to assign a response that will help the teacher assess the students' mastery of the targeted skill or strategy

A Sample Minilesson on Summarization

When I teach summarization, I always differentiate between fiction and nonfiction summaries. I teach students the SWBS (Somebody Wanted But So) strategy for fiction. This strategy focuses student attention on the important structure of fiction. The first *S* (*Somebody*) requires the student to identify the main character in the reading that day. The *W* (*Wanted*) asks the student to identify that character's goal. The *B* (*But*) identifies the conflict, the person, or situation that stands between the character and the goal. The *S* (*So*) focuses the reader's attention on what that character did or tried to do to overcome the problem. For nonfiction, I use the 5Ws and an H strategy (Who, What, When, Where, Why, How). This strategy cues the reader to identify the important information in nonfiction. To use these strategies this well takes time—and I am not about to rush through the strategy in a minilesson and then ask students to do it.

If I have already spent the time necessary to teach these two strategies and when to use each one and I am confident that the *majority* of the students are ready to try it alone, I might choose summarization as my response focus for the week. My minilesson would then go like this:

> *Students, we have spent a lot of time learning about summaries. Who can remind me how summarizing helps us as readers?* [Wait for answer.]
>
> *That's right. Summarizing helps us take all the information we have read and reduce it to just the important parts. We know, as readers, that some things in the text are more important than others.*
>
> *Do we summarize fiction and nonfiction in the same way?* [Wait for answer.]
>
> *That's right. When we summarize fiction, we want to focus on the main characters, their problems, and the solutions to those problems. When we summarize nonfiction, we focus on the what or who is important and why.*
>
> *When you finish reading today, I'm going to ask you to write a summary of what you read. If you are reading fiction, please use the SWBS strategy to summarize. If you are reading nonfiction, please use the 5Ws and an H strategy. The two posters at the front of the room are there to help you in case you've forgotten exactly what to do and you should also have notes on, and examples of, each strategy in your reading folders.*
>
> *So, as you're reading today, you will be focusing on either the important elements of character, problem, and solution if you are reading fiction or on who or what is important and why if you are reading nonfiction.*
>
> *I'm going to give each of you three small sticky notes to use to mark places you think will be important to go back to as you write your summaries. If you need more, just let me know. I'm carrying extras with me as I walk the room today.*
>
> *Go ahead and log in on your reading logs for today. Just stop me as I go by if you have any questions.*

Notice that the *students* have been asked to supply the initial information so that it is clear that most of them understand the skill or strategy they are being asked to apply. They have also been reminded of two extra places to go for help if the teacher is not available—posters at the front of the room that were created as the strategies were taught and notes in their reading notebooks to which they can refer as needed. By using sticky notes to mark information, the flow of their reading is not interrupted during the independent reading time. Those who know exactly what to do have not been kept from getting right to their reading by asking if there are any questions. Instead, it has been made clear that the teacher is available for any individual questions the students might have.

Targeted Conferencing

I wish I were such an amazing teacher that all my deep teaching and a quick reminder would be enough to make every student successful on any skill or strategy I am targeting, but I haven't reached quite that level of competence yet—nor has anyone else I know. Some students will just take longer to understand than others. As teachers work with students, it is important for them to predict who will be confused when it comes time for the response. Conferencing's purpose will be to unscramble some of the thinking for these students.

Let's suppose that Monica still struggles with summaries. Today, she is reading an *Amber Brown* book, so she will need to use the SWBS strategy, which she hasn't mastered yet.

Because she is clearly still struggling with the strategy, it is important to plan to conference with Monica today. Since the focus will be on her ability to summarize, she will need time to read before the conference. Other students can be checked on for about 15 minutes, and then Monica will have read enough to be ready to talk. A conference with her might start like this:

> *I see you're on page 43 of your Amber Brown book. This is the second Amber Brown book you've read. You must really be enjoying them! Can you tell me what's happened so far in the book?*

The chances are that Monica's answer will either be skeletal or overembellished because she is still learning to summarize. The rest of the conference will address whichever extreme she is presenting. If her answer is skeletal, she will be asked for specifics. If her answer is overembellished, she will be asked which of those details are the most important. Before the conference ends, the teacher must talk her through today's response, being sure she understands how the information she has given would fit into the SWBS format.

Sometimes, just one individual conference is enough to help a student who has been struggling clear up any misconceptions—but those cases are rare. When students are confused, it usually takes time to straighten out their thinking. If teachers have done their best with each child each day, it is pointless to agonize over the fact that a seemingly brilliant intervention didn't result in a changed student. It is also unconscionable to give up in frustration and just let a student continue to be confused. After looking at what is written today and noticing where confusion still lies, it will be necessary to go back tomorrow with one new thing to say that may be exactly what the student needs to hear. Teachers then must remember the hint that worked—and use it again and again with other students who are similarly confused, some of whom will get it from that one comment and some of whom won't. Each student is an individual—and student thinking is also individualized. The teachers must do the best they can each day for each student—and get up tomorrow and start again.

Taking Conference Notes

When I taught middle school, I saw 150 students over 2 days. There was no way I could remember what I said to each one. Now, the number of students I see in a day varies—but I still can't remember everything I've said without taking notes. An efficient note-taking system is an important element of planning and implementing good instruction.

I have tried a number of systems—random notes on notebook paper that I later transcribe and transfer to folders, separate sheets of paper in a notebook for each student. Neither of these systems worked for me because they were too cumbersome. God bless the teacher I met in a workshop who suggested taking notes on address labels.

The procedure is simple: 2 × 4 inch address labels from the local office supply store are placed on a clipboard. On each label, a student's name is written so that there is a label for each student. This guarantees that the teacher will conference with each student at some time over about a 3-day period. Even the strongest readers will need to be given attention.

At the start of the conference, the day's date, the book the student is reading, and the page on which the student is working is written on the address label bearing that student's name. This helps teachers keep track of students who have changed books, as well as those who are making good progress through the texts they have chosen. During the conference, notes are taken on what has been discussed and on any action that needs to be taken before the student is seen again (Appendix C).

After a label has been filled with information, it is peeled off the sheet and put on a sheet of paper with the student's name at the top. These sheets can be kept in a notebook or in file folders so they can be found easily. By reviewing everything written on these labels, student progress can be assessed and future instruction planned. These individual sheets are also invaluable when conducting parent conferences or meeting with other educators about students whose progress is an area of concern.

Time for Response

Yes, students will be asked to respond to their reading—but it is important that the response not interfere with the reading itself. If students have to stop reading and write what they're thinking, they have just lost valuable time. Readers who are trying to catch up don't have this time to lose.

Response notes at the end of independent reading time should take no more than 5 minutes. Students need to write just enough for the teacher to see if they have understood the skill or strategy targeted that day. They don't need to write an essay—just a few quick notes. Later, they might gather all these response together and write some sort of literary essay, but not at the end of their reading time.

If time is tight, the notes can always be written for homework. The next day, students can put their assignment on the lefthand corner of their desks as they begin independent reading. Conference time then begins with the teacher walking through the room and checking these responses.

Some of the students won't have a response. This is the only time teachers should ever ask students to stop reading. These students should be asked to stop what they are doing and write what was assigned from the day before. Five minutes is enough time to do that, and when the 5 minutes are up, the teacher should return to the students' desks and check their responses.

Not doing a note-taking assignment should never be an option. The information from the notes is too critical for these assignments to be ignored. If students don't do the work, they will not learn.

Notes have one purpose—to help teachers assess student understanding of a critical skill or strategy. If students can successfully demonstrate the skill or apply the strategy while they are working independently in a text they have chosen because *they* want to read it, the teacher can rest assured that these young readers have mastered the content that was taught.

The Adventure of Teaching

I often think about the pitifully ignored teacher in the movie *Ferris Bueller's Day Off,* who stands at the front of the room asking inane questions and droning, "Anybody? Anybody?" as students sleep through the class and he answers his own stupid questions. What a way to spend a career!

For me, teaching is a thrill ride every day. No two years, no two classes, and no two students are ever alike, and I must constantly change my approach and my focus to meet the needs of the individuals with whom I am privileged to work each day. Every single day, I learn more about my students, more about reading, more about teaching, and more about myself by confronting the problems my students present and finding ways to help *them* solve them.

Supported independent reading is the key to giving students ownership of their reading. By helping students learn to recognize a problem and know that *they* have the power to solve it, teachers have given them a critical power, the power to control their own learning—not just for today, but for a lifetime.

References

Allington, R. L. (2001). *What really matters for struggling readers: Designing research-based programs.* New York: Addison-Wesley.

Calkins, L. M. (2001). *The art of teaching reading.* New York: Addison-Wesley.

Gallagher, M., & Pearson, P. D. (1983). The instruction of reading comprehension. *Contemporary Educational Psychology, 8,* 317–344.

Hughes, J. (Director). (1986). *Ferris Bueller's day off.* [Motion picture] United States: Paramount Pictures.

Jensen, E. (1998). *Teaching with the brain in mind.* Alexandria, VA: Association for Supervision and Curriculum Development.

Krashen, S. D. (2004). *The power of reading: Insights from research.* Portsmouth, NH: Heinemann.

McKenna, M. C. (2001). Development of reading attitudes. In L. Verhoeven & C. Snow (Eds.), *Literacy and motivation: Reading engagement in individuals and groups* (pp. 135–158). Mahwah, NJ: Lawrence Erlbaum.

Routman, R. (2000). *Conversations.* Portsmouth, NH: Heinemann.

Chapter 3

Engaging Readers

Beware the "Field of Dreams."

In this 1989 movie fantasy, Kevin Costner carves a baseball diamond into his cornfield because a mystical voice has assured him that "if you build it, they will come." It is just as fanciful for teachers to believe that giving students 30 minutes every day to read will insure that they do so.

Some students *will* read—the ones who clutch the latest *Harry Potter* book tightly to their chests on the first day of school or who leap with enthusiasm when a new book club flyer arrives. These students already see themselves as capable readers and have already found joy on the printed page. Look past them to the boy in the next row who carries that same *Harry Potter* book but never opens it. See the girl in the corner who spends 20 of the 30 minutes drawing a beautiful story map—but spends only 10 minutes or less actually reading. Notice the class behavior problem who not only has no book to read, but has no intention of doing so anyway. And while you're noticing, please look at the quiet, compliant child sitting in the center of the room dutifully holding a book whose pages never turn.

Those of us who teach at the intermediate- and middle school levels deal with disengaged readers every day. Some of them may read just well enough to pass a standardized test or to function in content-area textbooks. But most of them read so little that they continue to fall farther and farther behind.

Redefining the Term *Reader*

For 18 years, I worked in an urban school district that is one of the most diverse in the country. The students not only came from all over the world and spoke dozens of different languages, but the majority of them also came from poverty. Most of the reluctant readers with whom I worked had no books in their homes and had no adult role models who read. Children were often left unsupervised—not because of negligent parents, but because of poorly paid ones. The parents often worked multiple jobs just to make ends meet—and sometimes the ends never quite matched up, so families moved continuously as they were evicted from one apartment complex after another. Books and magazines were often considered luxuries that the family just couldn't afford. Most of the struggling students with whom I worked owned no books, had no library cards, and saw no one who read outside of school. They could name no one in their life who was a reader.

Once students such as these enter school, many of them struggle with reading from the beginning. They are already behind children whose parents have read to them, taken them to the library, and given them books as gifts. These activities communicate that reading is important, that it is a pleasurable activity. When students equate reading with the love and care of a parent or other significant adult, the positive emotions they associate with the reading experience help lead them to reading success. These students often zoom past those with no reading role models—and those left behind view themselves more and more as reading failures. Without a fundamental belief in the value of reading, students will lose their desire to do the hard work that catching up will entail.

Struggling students are the ones who are pulled into guided reading groups that focus on what good readers do. These groups are important and serve as effective interventions for students who *want* to be good readers—but what if they don't want to be readers at all?

Our first goal needs to be giving all the students in our classes a clear vision of what it means to be a *reader*—not just a *good* reader, but a true reader. Plenty of people in this world are good readers—but they never choose to read. Teachers should want more for their students.

A Lesson to Build the Concept of *Reader*

One of the first lessons I teach each school year is one designed to clearly illustrate what I mean by the term *reader*. A piece of chart paper is posted at the front of the room as students enter. On it is written "What is a reader?" and under that is the stem sentence: "Readers...."

I begin class by letting students contribute ideas to this chart. Typically, students will tell me that readers can read all the words, that they understand what they read, that they use their strategies. In this age of No Child Left Behind (2001), students now add that readers can read fluently when they read out loud. Usually, someone will add that readers read a lot—I'm always happy to add that one to the chart. As students offer ideas for me to write on the chart paper, I begin to get a picture of their previous experiences with, and expectations for, reading.

Once I have collected the student ideas, I tell them proudly that I am a *reader*—dramatically emphasizing the last word in the sentence. I tell them I am going to talk to them about what I do that makes me claim that title—and that after that, we'll see if there's anything we need to add to our chart.

At this point I drag—and I do mean *drag*—a huge canvas bag out from behind my desk. The bag is one I was given during a social studies textbook adoption, and it holds a huge collection of texts. In the bag are magazines, the arts section of the Sunday paper, children's books, adult books, professional books, and graduate textbooks. In the bag are books I love and even those I hate. I sit down in a chair and begin to talk about all the things I am reading right now.

I start with the magazines. With each example I draw from the bag, I clearly and casually state exactly why I read that text. I have issues of *People* (I read that for fun to catch up on celebrity gossip), *Texas Monthly* and *Vanity Fair* (I love the writing and the articles are always interesting), *Chile* (I find recipes here), and *The Reading Teacher* (I want to be a better teacher every day). Then, I show the Sunday arts section and discuss how it helps me decide what book I want to read next, adding, "And I read a *lot* of books! Let me show you."

I talk about how I read a lot of different things all at the same time—and tell them that my husband doesn't understand this at all. He thinks I should finish one book before I start another—but, then, he is not a reader!

I start with the young adult books I'm actually reading at the time—the one I've just finished, the one I'm reading now, and the one I have chosen to read next. I refer back to *The Reading Teacher* and the Sunday paper as places I get ideas for what young adult books to read—but tell them that I make most of my choices because a student has recommended a book to me. This fall, I had just finished reading *Chasing Vermeer* by Blue Balliett (2005)—and I loved it. I did such a good job of selling that book that I have now had to buy several more copies as students borrowed the ones I had. I talked about that book, about *The Young Man and the Sea* by Rodman Philbrick (2004), that I was reading at the time, and about *The Schwa Was Here* by Neal Shusterman (2004), that I was planning to read next. All of these books were on our state's award list for this year. I try to show various kinds of books and even talk briefly about genre. Again, I talk about my purpose in reading these books—that I want to be familiar with books that I can recommend to students, plus I truly enjoy young adult fiction.

Next, I show the adult books I'm reading—both fiction and nonfiction. This fall, I was reading an Anne River Siddons novel—that one for pure escape and because she's one of my favorite authors—and *Gilead* by Marilynne Robinson (2004) because it won the Pulitzer Prize. I had *The Known World* by Edward P. Jones (2004) waiting in the wings; it, too, has won the Pulitzer. I talk a little bit about reading prize-winning books—that sometimes they take longer to get into because they have deep character development. This, of course, is true not only for adult books, but for children's books as well.

Then, I start on the nonfiction. This year, I pulled out the tour book for the Virgin Islands I'm reading to be ready for the cruise my husband and I will take this winter, *Rise of the Vulcans* by James Mann (2004), that I bought because I heard it discussed on a Sunday morning news program, and Anna Quindlen's (2004) *Imagined London,* which I found sitting at the edge of an aisle in Barnes & Noble. That book ties together two of my loves—London and the literature set there.

The next books from the bag are the professional books I'm reading. These look very different from the other books because a variety of adhesive "flags" protrude from many of the pages. My friends make fun of all the flags I use, wondering how they can be helpful when I use so many. But they *are* helpful to me—I can go back to those and revisit ideas I want to remember. These books are also highlighted because I own them. This gives me a chance to talk about how I have to *own* books—not just borrow them or check them out from the library. I want the books to be *mine*!!!! I want to write in them and bend the pages, take as long as I want to finish them, and reread them whenever I get the urge.

That gives me a chance to show my very well-worn copy of *Wuthering Heights*. This is my all-time favorite book, and I'm sure I've read it at least 50 times. I mention other books that I have reread—*To Kill a Mockingbird, Gone with the Wind*. Truly fantastic stories are worth revisitng.

This leads me to two books I didn't actually read—*The Corrections* by Jonathan Franzen (2002) and *The Life of Elizabeth* by Alison Weir (1999). I bought the Franzen book because of Oprah—and I really tried to read it. I read over 100 pages before I decided I just didn't like it enough to finish. I didn't care about any of the characters—I found all of them annoying—and

Franzen's writing style just wasn't to my taste. I know several people w[ho]
and loved this book, but it just wasn't for me.

The Weir book I bought because it is on one of my favorite topics—Quee[n]
Elizabeth I. I have read a lot of books about her and always yearn to know
more. She was strong at a time when that wasn't a quality that was admired in
a woman—and she lived life on her own terms despite a tragic childhood and
numerous assassination plots. But this book just had too many intricate details for me. I got bogged down in all the pages-long descriptions of feasts and
political documents. Again, I read nearly half the book before I decided it
would be one I wouldn't finish.

Students are always very surprised to learn that I don't finish every book I
start. I believe that is an important point to make. When they begin their
independent reading, they, too, are going to want to abandon books. I make
sure I give good, clear reasons why I chose the book and why I decided not to
finish it. If they want to make the same choice, they need to provide the same
types of information—why they chose the book, what they expected it to be,
and why the book didn't live up to their expectations. Just telling me, "It's
boring," is not going to fly. This also gives me the chance to stress the fact that
I want them to *enjoy* what they read.

The last books I show them are the ones I've had to buy for graduate classes.
Like the other nonfiction books, these are decorated with flags. These, however, are books I didn't choose to read—someone else required them. I spend
some time talking about how much harder it is to read a book I didn't choose
myself. Someone else chose it—someone who will expect me to be able to prove
that I not only read it, but understood it.

My favorite book to use for this part of the lesson is my statistics textbook.
Reading that was a tiring experience for me. I had no statistics classes as an
undergraduate and had, in fact, avoided math classes as much as possible. I tell
the kids I had to be in a quiet place where no one would disturb me and had to
read and reread sections numerous times. I tell them that sometimes no matter
how hard I tried, nothing made sense—at which time I would go find my
husband, the engineer, and have him explain parts to me. I *couldn't* abandon
this book (though I really wanted to)—and the reading was very hard for me.
I had to go to someone who knew more to help me.

Students are, of course, surprised to find out that I sometimes need help
with my reading—but it is an important point to make. They need to understand that a reader will find ways to make text make sense—if that fits their
purpose for reading.

Once the last book is out of the canvas bag, I look at the students and say,
"Now you can see why I call myself a *reader*!" At that point, we revisit the chart.

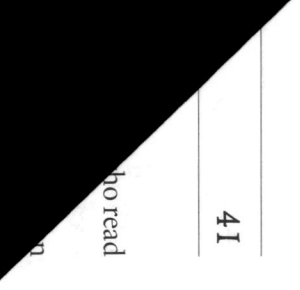

ng Independent Readers

llowing are the things the students will add—
 o the ideas we collected earlier:

rent kinds of texts.

 rpose for their reading—and read for many

more than one book at a time.

- Readers finish books.
- Readers like to own books.
- Readers know what they will read next.
- Readers get ideas about what to read next from magazines, newspapers, television, awards lists, book stores, and other readers.
- Readers have favorite books and authors.
- Readers reread books they love.
- Readers don't finish books they don't like—but they give them a good try first and know exactly why they didn't like them.
- Readers know what to expect from the type of book they're reading.
- Readers read books they didn't choose differently from books they chose for themselves.
- Readers slow down and reread when the text is hard.
- Readers ask for help if the text just isn't making sense.

This chart becomes a basis for many more lessons—all directed at engaging students with their reading. It stays up in the classroom throughout the year—and is referenced often when talking to students about both the good and bad decisions they are making as readers. My goal is not to create *good* readers—that will take care if itself if I can create *true* readers who read for joy.

Teaching for Engagement

McKenna (2001) points out that three specific factors shape students' engagement with texts: their previous reading experiences, their expectations for the reading, and the culture around them. All three factors need to be addressed if teachers want a classroom filled with willing readers.

Previous Reading Experiences

Although some try to pretend otherwise, struggling students know they are poor readers. They equate this lack of skill with lack of intelligence rather than lack of practice and motivation. Experiences from their pasts have shaped their images of themselves—and by taking an honest look at these experiences, students can start to understand that letting go of negative experiences can make their future look very different from their past.

Early in the year, teachers should ask students to write reading autobiographies (Fig. 3:1). The purpose of this assignment is to ask students to reflect on their previous experiences so that they understand why they feel the way they do about reading. Many disengaged readers just know that they hate reading—they really aren't sure why. By taking a look at their reading histories, they can begin to see where experiences have shaped their attitudes. Then, their teachers can work to provide more positive experiences with texts.

Teachers should first share their own experiences, openly and honestly. The writing should be conversational, since students will be sharing draft writing, not a finished piece. It should be clear to students that the purpose of the writing is to help the teacher get to know them better as readers.

---

1. What memories do you have about reading and books from before you ever started school? It's okay if you don't have any, but mention that you don't.

2. Do you remember learning how to read? When? Was it hard or easy?

3. What have your experiences with reading in school been like? Tell the good and the bad—both are very important.

4. How have you felt about the read-aloud times in your classrooms? Are there any books you have enjoyed?

5. Do you have a favorite book or author? Talk about them.

6. What do you feel are your strengths as a reader? You have them, you know! Find at least one—but hopefully more!

7. What would you like to be able to do as a reader? Give me some good ideas on how to help you.

Figure 3:1 What to include in your history as a reader.

Expectations for Reading

The expectations students have for texts are critical to whether they enjoy or dread the reading experience (McKenna, 2001). Two verbs should shape students' expectations for reading; they should read books they *understand* and *enjoy*. They must learn to choose books for independent reading that are at the correct level and that are interesting to them. Otherwise, students who are behind will not be likely to spend the extra time it will take for them to catch up. Allington (2001) contends that "... engagement in reading has been found to be the most powerful instructional activity for fostering reading growth" (p. 37).

Teachers need to continually reiterate to students that every book they choose for themselves should be something in which they are interested that is at a manageable reading level. Disengaged readers are usually not even aware of all the different types of books available, since many of them have not ever chosen books they actually intended to read. Kylene Beers (1998) reminds us that struggling readers see the library as an alien environment that they have no desire to navigate. A true reader sees time spent in a library as an invigorating experience; students who do not choose to read see it as wasted time.

Choice is critical to student success and essential for motivation. In fact, Daniels and Bizar (2005) stress that students must learn "to make meaningful decisions and choices, living with all the consequences that choice entails" (p. 26). But students cannot be expected to make informed choices if they are not aware of all the choices at hand. If their choices are ever going to matter, students who expect the library to be the place where they grab a random book from the shelf and later pretend to read it must be taught instead to expect to find a book there that they will love.

Early in the school year, students need to be dazzled by the endless variety of books available to them. They should hold, preview, and skim through books from the classroom and school libraries, books that they can actually access when independent reading begins. The teacher's goals must include clarifying and changing student expectations for reading.

Skilled readers know what to expect when they open a mystery or a science fiction novel; they know that nonfiction texts look very different from those in the fiction section—and are read differently as well. This is one reason why many struggling readers, as Sibberson and Szymusiak (2003) point out, are confused from the moment they begin reading. Without a clear understanding of how texts are structured and what elements define a genre, they have no idea how to approach text.

Students need a cursory tour of these reading destinations so that they know what genres might interest them. Teachers can help by exploring the popular genres of realistic fiction, mystery, suspense, fantasy, science fiction, historical fiction, biography, and informational text one at a time in a series of lessons. Each day's lesson should include what to expect from each genre and actual books that the students can explore. Students can hold their thinking by making booklets or folders in which they take notes on the characteristics of the various genres, specific titles and authors who write each type of book, and information on how to find the book in the library. Taking this organizer with them will help them be more successful on their trips to the library.

This series of lessons must include explicit instruction on the organization of the library and on the information found on the spines of library books. Students must understand that:

- Fiction will be in a separate section from nonfiction.
- Fiction titles are arranged alphabetically by the author's last name, so they must know that name.
- Biographies are arranged alphabetically by the subject's last name, not the author's.
- Nonfiction is arranged numerically.
- The nonfiction numbers have meaning.
- The letters and numbers on the spines of books are there to help us find them easily in the library.

Students should see and touch as many books as possible each day, so the teacher should combine short book talks with what Janet Allen (2000) calls a book pass. Each day should focus on a new genre.

A Series of Lessons Aimed at Changing Expectations

Realistic fiction is a good starting place for these lessons, since this is the easiest genre for students to access. The teacher should place an assortment of realistic fiction books at stations in the classroom. Titles at each station should represent a wide range of reading levels so that even the most challenged readers can find books at their level. Accelerated Reader lists, the backs of books, Web sites, and the school librarian are excellent sources to use to establish the levels and to be sure currently popular titles are included.

The teacher should choose three titles at varying levels each day to highlight. On the first day, the teacher will need to discuss the term *genre*—that it just means "a certain kind of book." Students need to understand that all books in a genre have common characteristics—and that by knowing what these characteristics are readers know what to expect when they read the book. All too often, teachers forget that understanding of genre is important prior knowledge for students to access before reading. As in any other instance, if students lack this knowledge, it must be built before students can be expected to read with understanding.

Together, the students and teacher build a chart of the characteristics of the genre being highlighted that day. Characteristics should center around what to expect in the characters, the setting, and the events. The teacher can use familiar movies or television shows to prompt student thinking. Historical fiction and science fiction will usually take more time because these genres are often so confusing for students.

When choosing books to highlight each day, the teacher should try to choose authors who have written several titles. Many reluctant readers' attitudes have changed with books by Andrew Clements or Barbara Park. Recurring characters, such as Junie B. Jones, and familiar settings, such as the school-centered stories of Andrew Clements, provide a degree of comfort for students as they grow as readers.

Each of the three books should be held up individually, starting with the easiest to read and ending with the most difficult. That distinction should be made quite clearly to the students, stressing again that their reading level is an indication only of how much time they have spent reading. Students may be really interested in books that are too hard for them at the moment, but they can be coached to consider those their target books—the ones they're working toward being able to read. Parts of each book should be read aloud so the students can get a sense of the author's style and the type of vocabulary and sentence structure used. The section chosen should whet student appetites and leave them wanting more (Fig. 3:2). These same books can be used during read-aloud time by reading only one chapter and then moving on. Students have been known to swarm the library wanting to check out books their teachers have quit reading at the very best part.

Once the day's book talks are finished, students should be given a book pass sheet (Appendix D) to guide their previewing of the books in the stations. Each book pass sheet should be copied on two sides so students have room for a number of titles. Students are then directed to inspect each book at their center and to fill in the columns of the book pass sheet for that book. They may then look at another book in the stack. Students record the titles of the books they want to read in their library guide booklet, being sure to include the author's last name.

Mystery/Suspense
Easy: 　*The Empty Envelope* by Ron Roy (1998) Chapter 2—9 pages 　*Cam Jansen and the Birthday Mystery* by David A. Adler (2002) Chapter 3—7 pages **Average:** 　*Stonewords* by Pam Conrad (1991) Chapter 2—11 pages 　*Ghosts beneath Our Feet* by Mary Downing Hahn (1995) Chapter 4—5 pages **Advanced:** 　*The Face on the Milk Carton* by Caroline B. Cooney (1991) Chapter 1—11 pages 　*The Other Side of Dark* by Joan Lowery Nixon (1987) Chapter 2—10 pages

Realistic Fiction
Easy: 　*Judy Moody* by Megan McDonald (2002) "Two Heads Are Better Than One"—16 pages 　*Junebug* by Alice Mead (1997) Chapter 1—7 pages **Average:** 　*Crash* by Jerry Spinelli (1996) Chapter 1—4 pages 　*Joey Pigza Swallowed the Key* by Jack Gantos (2000) "Off the Wall"—4 pages **Advanced:** 　*The Same Stuff as Stars* by Katherine Paterson (2002) "Hansel and Grizzle"—10 pages 　*Walk Two Moons* by Sharon Creech (1996) "The Chickabiddy Starts a Story"—6 pages

Fantasy
Easy: 　*The Twits* by Roald Dahl (1998) "The Glass Eye" and "The Frog"—6 pages 　*The Castle in the Attic* by Elizabeth Winthrop (1986) Chapter 3—9 pages **Average:** 　*Ella Enchanted* by Gail Carson Levine (1997) Chapter 1—7 pages 　*The Tale of Despereaux* by Kate DiCamillo (2003) Chapter 3—6 pages **Advanced:** 　*Redwall* by Brian Jacques (1998) Chapter 5—5 pages 　*Artemis Fowl* by Eoin Colfer (2001) Chapter 1—15 pages

Figure 3:2 Some recommended chapters for engaging read alouds.

The book pass sheets are turned in at the end of the period and provide valuable information about each reader. Which books were rated as interesting? Which were too hard? Teachers should keep notes on students' reactions to the books so that they will be able to help them find a book that is perfect for them.

After discussing the fiction genres, teachers can move on to biography, taking the time to draw the parallel between the structure of fiction and the structure of biographies. Both have a narrative structure that centers on people—fictional characters or live human beings. Both present information arranged in some type of time order.

Biographies, however, have a very different purpose. Authors write fiction to engage readers in a story; they write biographies to share important details about real people's lives. The events in biographies are not likely to be as elaborately developed as those in fiction, since the author's purpose is to inform rather than to entertain. This is also an excellent opportunity for teachers to point out the charts, graphs, and timelines that are included in many of the current biographies written for children. These nonfiction conventions are designed to make the information easier to access.

Biographies form the bridge between fiction and nonfiction. It is essential, particularly for struggling readers, to highlight nonfiction texts if teachers want to motivate every reader in the room. Many students, particularly boys and English-language learners, find nonfiction more compelling than fiction. Current series on high-performance vehicles and military weapons can often catch the attention of even the most reluctant boy, and language learners approach nonfiction with more background knowledge than they do fiction set in contemporary or historic America. If an entire week is spent on nonfiction, it is time well spent.

On the first day spent highlighting nonfiction, teachers should spend a great deal of time explicitly detailing the differences between fiction and nonfiction. Always, it comes back to author's purpose. Even in books like Laurence Pringle's (1997) fascinating *An Extraordinary Life: The Story of a Monarch Butterfly,* the 1998 Orbis Pictus award winner, the author's purpose is still to provide the reader with information about a topic—in this case, monarch butterflies.

When reading fiction, readers should focus on the narrative elements of character, setting, events, problem, and solution; when reading nonfiction, readers should look for the important points authors are making about their chosen topic. What do readers know after reading that they didn't know before? This overview should be developed throughout the year by using nonfiction texts as read alouds and offering examples of the various text structures. But for now, the idea of nonfiction is merely being planted in readers' minds; later, lessons will nurture that seed and prompt it to grow.

Teachers should also spend time during this introduction showing students how to preview a nonfiction book. For fiction books, they will look at the inside fly leaves, the backs of books, and chapter titles. For nonfiction books, they will need to flip through the chapters, noticing the headings, pictures, and graphics. They will need to look carefully at the table of contents and may even want to examine the index in the back. Teachers should take the time to point out that nonfiction titles will contain what is called specialized vocabulary, words that are only used when discussing whatever the topic might be. Often, there is a glossary in the back to help or the words may be defined within the text.

Students need to understand how to locate nonfiction in the library. They don't need to memorize the Dewey decimal system, but they do need to understand that the books are grouped together by type. Unlike fiction—where readers might have to go all over the section hunting various authors of mysteries—in nonfiction, all the similar books are grouped together. This makes even finding a book easier for reluctant students; if they know what interests them and where it can be found, they can return again and again to the same spot until they have read everything available there. The library, then, becomes a less threatening place.

Students enjoy the challenge of discovering the focus of the various numbered sections on their own. As they work at stations, the books at each station should all be from the same numbered section of the library. Besides completing their book pass sheets, students are also asked to discover why these books would all be found in the same section of the library. Class discussions after these examinations can result in a student-friendly guide to the Dewey decimal system that can become a class reference all year.

There is no way to accurately describe the excitement that fills the room when students are exploring nonfiction. They discover titles such as *Oh, Yuck! The Encyclopedia of Everything Nasty* by Joy Masoff (2000), *The World's Fastest Trucks: Built for Speed* by Glen and Karen Bledsoe (2002), Monica Hughes's *Creepy Creatures* series, or the ever-popular books of world records. During these book passes, the only redirection teachers will normally need to give is to ask students to give up a book because someone else wants to see it. Students want to begin reading the books right then and there.

While these initial lessons consume the first 2–3 weeks of the school year, they are an essential key to student engagement. By showcasing the various types of books available to them, clarifying what to expect from each type of book, and giving students chances to actually explore the books themselves, teachers have created a culture of excitement centered around learning. Because they have had a chance to write down titles of books they would actually like to read, students become motivated to choose their own books and to do so with success. Jobe and Dayton-Sakari (1999) remind teachers, "Choice is power. In a literacy interaction, whoever picks what to read holds the power and the other person is just along for the ride" (p. 35). Teachers should strive to put their students in the driver's seat—not just for a day, but for a lifetime.

The Classroom Culture

The older students get, the more important their peers become. Fitting in becomes their ultimate goal. The research on motivation reminds us that two essential keys to increasing reading motivation are fostering an attachment to the others in the room (Lyons, 2003) and centering the classroom culture around literacy (McKenna, 2001). The teacher is instrumental in building this culture.

On the first day of school, when students enter the room, students should find themselves engulfed in a world centered on reading. Books should be everywhere—lined up along the chalktrays, organized in shelves and baskets along the walls, and placed in stacks or book boxes in the center of desks. The first thing teachers should do with their classes each year is read to them.

My favorite read aloud for the first day of school is *Book* by George Ella Lyon (1999). This engaging picture book uses a series of metaphors to show what books offer to dedicated readers. It sets the stage for a school year to be spent reading books we love. Another picture book by Lyon (1998), *A Sign*, can preface a discussion of why authors write books and how they attempt to connect to readers. Students often forget that at some point in time, another human being actually sat down and put the words they are reading on paper, anticipating that they would someday be read and enjoyed. Other good books that set the stage for a reading community are *Wolf!* by Becky Bloom (1999) and *Edward and the Pirates* by David McPhail (1997). Although students may well have heard of these books before, the ideas they present about reading's place in students' lives is well worth revisiting.

The teacher is only one person in the classroom; the actual community must include each individual student. It is not enough for teachers to be readers. They must help the students see themselves as readers as well.

The greatest tool at teachers' disposal to accomplish this goal is classroom talk. From the first day of school, students should be greeted in the morning and asked about their reading. As they enter the classroom on that first day, the teacher should ask, "Did you read any good books over the summer?" These conversations are casual and should become a normal part of the school day.

Teachers should constantly talk to students about texts. If they read something students might like, they should recommend it or, if possible, put the actual book or article in students' hands. If there are books on student desks, teachers should ask about them—particularly if the teacher has not previously read them. A great conversation starter is, "I haven't read this one. Is it any good?" Teachers can then pick up the book and read the back, demonstrating one more time how a reader previews books. If the teacher *has* read the book, asking what part the student is on, and possibly teasing them with what's coming next, can build a bond between teacher and student.

A reluctant student with whom I worked was reading *The Dollhouse Murders* by Betty Ren Wright (1995). He had pulled the book from the classroom library, intrigued by both the title and a teacher recommendation. Wright, however, takes a long time setting up the story and getting to what the student was waiting for—the scary part. I merely asked, "Have the dolls started moving in the dollhouse yet? It's coming up soon, you know." That was all it took to keep him reading.

Centering teacher-to-student talk on books gives teachers an opportunity to connect to each of their students, even the more unruly ones. A short, informal conversation about books with the student who, yesterday, spent the entire day acting out can change the tone of student–teacher relationships and clearly communicate that today is a new day, and a student's growth as a reader is more important than classroom disruptions. Books are nonthreatening and impersonal. Conversations can be meaningful, and through time, a sense of trust can be developed. These conversations should be one-on-one, a personal moment in each day for each child. They can happen anywhere—at the classroom door, at student desks, in the hallway, at lunch. But they should happen regularly for every student.

As teachers continue to hold conversations with students about books, a strange phenomenon occurs. Other students begin to join in. They eavesdrop and become interested in what is being said. Suddenly, they jump in with comments like, "I've read that book before—it's great!" or "Can I read that book when you're finished?" The stage has been set for a classroom community that focuses on reading.

When these informal discussions start, it is time to introduce the Books I Want to Read sheet (Appendix E). These sheets are kept in student reading folders and checked regularly. Teachers should check to see which students are actually listing titles there—and if they are following up by actually reading the book. When students are planning what they will read next, they are becoming true readers.

Like any good stage director, once the stage is set, teachers can hide in the wings. They can step back and watch *students* having conversations about books as they make recommendations to each other and excitedly discuss the best parts of books. A culture centered on reading has been built—and the momentum will be unstoppable.

References

Allen, J. (2000). *Yellow brick roads: Shared and guided paths to independent reading 4–12*. Portland, ME: Stenhouse.

Allington, Richard L. (2001). *What really matters for struggling readers*. New York: Addison-Wesley.

Beers, K. (1998). Choosing not to read: Understanding why some middle schoolers just say no. In K. Beers & B. G. Samuels (Eds.), *Into focus: Understanding and creating middle school readers* (pp. 37–63). Norwood, MA: Christopher-Gordon.

Daniels, H., & Bizar, M. (2005). *Teaching the best practice way: Methods that matter, K–12*. Portland, ME: Stenhouse.

Jobe, R., & Dayton-Sakari, M. (1999). *Reluctant readers: Connecting students and books for successful reading experiences*. Markham, Ontario, Canada: Pembroke.

Lyons, C. A. (2003). *Teaching struggling readers*. Portsmouth, NH: Heinemann.

McKenna, M. C. (2001). Development of reading attitudes. In L. Verhoeven & C. Snow (Eds.), *Literacy and motivation: Reading engagement in individuals and groups* (pp. 135–158). Mahwah, NJ: Lawrence Erlbaum.

Robinson, P. A. (Director). (1989). *Field of dreams*. [Motion picture] United States: Universal Studios.

Sibberson, F., & Szymusiak, K. (2003). *Still learning to read: Teaching students in grades 3–6*. Portland, ME: Stenhouse.

United States Department of Education. (2001). Elementary and secondary education act. Retrieved June 15, 2006, from http://www.ed.gov/policy/elsec/leg/esea02/beginning.html#sec1.

Trade Books Cited

Adler, D. A. (2002). *Cam Jansen and the birthday mystery*. East Rutherford, NJ: Puffin.

Balliett, B. (2005). *Chasing Vermeer*. New York: Scholastic.

Bledsoe, G., & Bledsoe, K. (2002). *The world's fastest truck (built for speed)*. Mankato, MN: Capstone.

Bloom, B. (1999). *Wolf!* New York: Scholastic.

Bronte, E. (1983). *Wuthering Heights*. New York: Bantam Classics.

Colfer, E. (2001). *Artemis fowl*. New York: Hyperion.

Conrad, P. (1991). *Stonewords*. New York: HarperCollins.

Cooney, C. B. (1991). *The face on the milk carton*. New York: Laurel Leaf.

Creech, S. (1996). *Walk two moons*. New York: HarperTrophy.

Dahl, R. (1998). *The twits.* London: Puffin.

DiCamillo, K. (2003). *The tale of despereaux.* New York: Scholastic.

Franzen, J. (2002). *The corrections.* New York: Picador.

Gantos, J. (2000). *Joey Pigza swallowed the key.* New York: HarperTrophy.

Hahn, M. D. (1995). *Ghosts beneath our feet.* New York: Scholastic.

Hughes, M. *The Creepy Creatures* series. Orlando, FL: Raintree.

Jacques, B. (1998). *Redwall.* New York: Ace.

Jones, E. P. (2004). *The known world.* New York: Amistad.

Lee, H. (1988). *To kill a mockingbird.* New York: Warner Books.

Levine, G. C. (1997). *Ella enchanted.* New York: HarperCollins.

Lyon, G. E. (1998). *A sign.* New York: Orchard.

Lyon, G. E. (1999). *Book.* New York: DK Children.

Mann, J. (2004). *The rise of the vulcans.* New York: Viking.

Masoff, J. (2000). *Oh, yuck! The encyclopedia of everything nasty.* New York: Workman.

McDonald, M. (2002). *Judy moody.* Cambridge, MA: Candlewick.

McPhail, D. (1997). *Edward and the pirates.* New York: Little, Brown.

Mead, A. (1997). *Junebug.* New York: Dell Yearling.

Mitchell, M. (1993). *Gone with the wind.* New York: Warner Books.

Nixon, J. L. (1987). *The other side of dark.* New York: Laurel Leaf.

Paterson, K. (2002). *The same stuff as stars.* New York: HarperTrophy.

Philbrick, R. (2004). *The young man and the sea.* New York: Scholastic.

Pringle, L. (1997). *An extraordinary life: The story of a monarch butterfly.* Fremont, CA: Orchard.

Quindlen, A. (2004). *Imagined London.* Washington, DC: National Geographic Society.

Robinson, M. (2004). *Gilead.* New York: Farrar, Straus & Giroux.

Roy, R. (1998). *The empty envelope.* New York: Random House Books for Young Readers.

Shusterman, N. (2004). *The schwa was here.* New York: Dutton Children's Books.

Spinelli, J. (1996). *Crash.* New York: Knopf.

Weir, A. (1999). *The life of Elizabeth I.* New York: Ballantine.

Winthrop, E. (1986). *The castle in the attic.* New York: Dell Yearling.

Wright, B. R. (1995). *The dollhouse murders.* New York: Scholastic.

Chapter 4

Organized Note Taking: A Tool for Making Thought Visible

When my older daughter was in middle school, I had the privilege of attending a breakfast where Joan Lowery Nixon was the keynote speaker. After the breakfast, this elegant author sat at a table and autographed books for us. I bought *A Family Apart* (1987), the first book in Nixon's *Orphan Train* series, and had Ms. Nixon autograph it for my daughter.

One night, as my husband and I sat watching TV, we heard our daughter's bedroom door open and heard the wailing begin. She stumbled down the stairs and stood at the door to our den, book in hand. "How could you do this to me?" she sobbed angrily. "Why didn't you tell me the family was going to be split apart at the end?"

That is a reader's response! It is that emotional involvement with an author's words that prompts those of us who love reading to spend a great deal of both our time and our money on a never-ending stream of texts. And it is that sort of personal involvement with an author's words that should be the goal of all our teaching. But before students can respond to words emotionally, they must first comprehend what they mean.

Developing the Abilities for Response

Teachers can't arm all our students with tear-jerking texts and wait for the sobbing to begin. They are working with developing readers whose progress must be monitored by a vigilant expert in the field. Because reading is an internal process, teachers must find a way to have students show them what is magically—or painfully—happening while they read. Before students can *respond* to texts, teachers must be certain that they have the skills and strategies to *understand* them.

The ultimate goal is to have students personally connect with what they are reading and respond, in what Rosenblatt (1995) terms, an aesthetic way. In this day of cable television, video games, MP3 players, and organized sports leagues, students have often spent much less time reading than students from previous eras—and much of that reading has been just going through the motions. Even older students are, very often, not ready to aesthetically respond to texts because they are still using all their mental energy just to understand them.

Before they can reach an aesthetic level in their reading, developing readers must understand the steps competent readers take to achieve that goal—and their teachers must be certain that the students in their classrooms have mastered the lower level comprehension skills that will make aesthetic responses possible.

The Reality of Reading Instruction

An administrator I know who clearly understands reading summed it up quite well one day: "Reading is messy." Unlike math, where students must master first addition and subtraction before they can possibly attempt multiplication and division, readers must use every skill at once to fully understand what they read. The proficient reader strategies highlighted by Keene and Zimmermann (1997) are essential tools for skilled readers, but, as Routman (2003) points out, they aren't used in isolation—they all run together. Skills such as determining the main idea, analyzing the character, and sequencing the events are all used simultaneously as well. If we narrow students' focus too much, they may view application of a strategy or mastery of a discrete skill as more important than the comprehension of the text itself. In reading, doing only one thing at a time can actually impede comprehension.

The content of a literacy curriculum changes very little over the years; main idea is main idea in every grade. However, the level of text complexity and vocabulary change dramatically as students move into higher levels of text. Some students will come with already high levels of proficiency and many of the requisite skills and strategies in place, while others will still have no clue.

The more experienced students are, the less time teachers should plan to spend providing whole-group instruction on the skills and strategies the students have been studying as part of the reading curriculum each year. Instead, students should be given more and more time to *practice* these skills and strategies in increasingly more complex texts. Teachers must help them learn to shape their thinking while reading so that they both understand and respond to the author's carefully chosen words. Well-designed graphic organizers provide an efficient, powerful tool for tracking and shaping student comprehension.

Keeping the Focus on Reading

During independent reading time, teachers are teaching *reading*, not writing. Writing ability often lags behind reading development (Bear, Invernizzi, Templeton, & Johnston, 2003), and students' lack of ability to express themselves in writing should not skew teachers' views of the thinking these students are actually doing as readers. For this reason, graphic organizers are better responses than open-ended questions. Later, open-ended questions, such as those recommended by Probst (1998), can be used to teach written response to texts—and the students can use their graphic organizer notes as prewriting.

Organized Note Taking

Organized notes are a reader's thinking made visible. They are tools a teacher uses to assess the progress of individual readers—but they will be ineffective unless they benefit the students as well. By asking students to take notes about what they have read, teachers should be trying to help them make sense of new information—but a carefully planned organizer will do more than that. It will be a vehicle for extending their thinking.

Effective notes must have four characteristics:

- They must target an essential skill or strategy that was reviewed in the day's minilesson.
- They must facilitate, rather than limit, students' comprehension of the texts they are reading.

- They must be short enough to be completed in approximately 5 minutes.
- They must be designed to enhance, and not interrupt, the reading experience.

Well-designed notes benefit both the students and the teacher. By holding the focus of the notes in their minds as they read, the students are practicing the invisible habits of skilled readers. By analyzing graphic organizers that take very little time to check, the teacher learns how well the students have mastered these skills and can prepare to move in with more support for the students who will need it.

Choosing the Target

My husband recently went on a hunting trip to a ranch with a managed herd. Each hunter was assigned to a guide whose job was to choose a deer for that hunter—and that was the *only* deer the hunter was allowed to shoot that day. In my blissful ignorance of all things hunting, I have no idea what criteria were used to select the ill-fated targets that weekend, but I do know that, in this way, the ranch manager controlled the quality of the herd.

Choosing the skill or strategy on which to focus student attention is ranch managing the reading in a classroom. Teachers must choose carefully, since by directing students' attention to a specific target that will focus their reading efforts for the day, the teacher is also controlling the quality of students' reading.

Several things should be considered when choosing a focus for the day's notes:

- What are you more concerned about at the moment—students' engagement with their texts or their understanding of them?
- What have you already taught in enough depth that you feel your students can apply it to their own reading?
- What kinds of texts are your students reading?
- Will one organizer work for the entire class or do you need to individualize more?
- How far are your students ready for you to push their thinking?
- Have you modeled what effective notes might look like with examples from your own reading during direct instruction?

Organized notes can focus on one of three areas: engagement, skills, or strategies. All are important, and the note taking assigned to students should represent a balance between these three areas.

Organizers that target engagement look at how involved the students are in their texts and invite them to connect with or to critique what they are reading. These organizers can also help readers think about their own reading—how they choose texts, how they overcome distractions.

Organizers targeting strategies focus on the tools proficient readers use to comprehend what they read (Keene & Zimmermann, 1997; Harvey & Goudvis, 2000). However, these strategies are a means to an end, not an end in themselves. Organizers focused on strategies help students learn to apply these tools to their own reading in an effort to better understand what they read.

Organizers targeting skills help teachers gauge where each student is in the course of developing the overall abilities proficient readers gain through strategy use. Educators have given these abilities labels and devised ways of testing them, all in an effort to determine whether or not readers are competent. But in the real world, people don't label these skills—they just exhibit them.

If I read a good editorial, I might look at my husband and say, "Did you read this editorial? It says that term limitation is the only way to diminish the influence of lobbyists." I have just stated the main idea. If my husband counters with, "How did they come up with that?" I might recite some details the author used to prove his point, first sorting out fact from opinion. When each of us decides in our own mind whether the editorial writer is a genius or an idiot, we have just made judgments. Students don't need to be able to label these skills—they just need to develop them.

Notes, Not Worksheets

Teaching students to organize their thinking with graphic organizers is very different from supplying students with xeroxed copies to use. The goal is to have the *students* own the strategy, not to have them depend on a teacher to provide them with a copied organizer that, in reality, becomes a glorified worksheet. Students need to learn the value and versatility of two- and three-column charts, lists, and webs and to even devise their own ways to use these for effective note taking. If someone else draws the graphic for them and runs them a copy, students are merely filling in the blanks. By drawing and labeling the organizers themselves, they are focusing on the type of thinking they will need to do to be successful and competent readers.

Real-world readers use strategies to skillfully read texts they have chosen themselves and in which they are truly engaged. All this happens at an almost unconscious level unless they have learned, as Keene and Zimmermann (1997) so beautifully illustrate, how to be metacognitive readers. Students need to learn the kinds of thinking their teachers do as readers that make them love reading as much as they do. The plan should always be to use the note-taking assignment to shape students' thinking in ways that will lead them to a higher level of involvement with the texts they have chosen.

A Week of Skill-Related Responses

Imagine that the teacher has just spent a great deal of time teaching character analysis, a skill that is tested on the state's test, and that it is important the students master it. The teacher has read aloud from picture books and chapter books alike, students have read passages in groups and analyzed the information presented about the characters in these brief excerpts, and they have read short stories from the literature book and practiced analyzing characters there. The majority of the students seem to have a general understanding of using characters' actions, thoughts, and words to infer what kinds of people they might be. The class has even built a word bank of words to describe characters and grouped them as complimentary and uncomplimentary. It is time to let the students practice on their own.

Because the teacher has seen this day coming, the last time the class went to the library, the students were told that they were going to need a fiction book as one of their reading choices. Although some of the students may be deeply involved in an informational text, they will need to put it aside for a few days while the class works on analyzing characters. After all, the teacher expects them to read from various genres—and they can still read their informational texts for homework reading.

By sometimes focusing on the skills needed for fiction and other times on those needed for nonfiction texts, the students' view of the world of texts is broadened. If they must have a certain type of book to complete the responses that week, they are, at least for a brief period of time, reading in a genre that they might not otherwise have chosen. In this way, the teacher is helping them discover new reading worlds that they may want to explore.

The current focus is on a skill—analyzing characters. A number of strategies support this skill—determining importance, synthesizing, and making connections, to name a few. Character analysis also requires a deep understanding of how texts are written—that authors plan events and conversations that will help readers learn the important things about each character. All of these things can serve as the focus of the students' organized notes.

The teacher should scaffold student understanding by gradually increasing the level of complexity of their thinking as students understand each step. To analyze a character, we must first collect information about that character, which requires the students to practice the strategy of determining what information about the character is important. The teacher might start by asking students to draw a character clue collection chart (Appendices D and E). This chart should already be familiar to them because the teacher will already have created one for a picture book during read-aloud time—and that chart will be displayed in the room.

During the minilesson, the teacher stands by the chart, holds up the picture book, and quickly reviews the process the class used that day—they noticed information, marked it with sticky notes, went back and added it to the chart, and then used that information to draw conclusions about the characters' personalities. Also, posted in the room should be the charts the class created with words to describe people—and the teacher will point those out as well, reminding students that these are good word banks to help jog their thinking. These charts will already have been used repeatedly as the class worked as a whole and in small groups. Nothing the teacher is asking the students to do will be new to them—it will just be their first chance to do it alone.

On Monday, the students will only begin collecting clues. Each student will be given several small sticky notes and asked to mark places where they think they got important information about their characters. They are not to stop and write until it is time for response; they are only to mark their places. The teacher should always carry extra sticky notes—some students may go a little crazy!

At the end of reading time, students will be asked to go back to their sticky notes and transfer the information to the chart in as few words as possible—just a phrase to help them remember. The teacher will again point to the chart created with the picture book where this type of note taking has already been modeled. When the teacher planned the direct instruction, this independent activity was always the goal—and its chance of success has been greatly increased by explicit teacher modeling of what the students are now being asked to do.

On Tuesday, the students will go one step further—they will not only collect information, but then choose three to five single words to describe the character as a person based on the collected clues. This will require them to synthesize the information they have gathered, another important strategy for comprehension. The teacher will remind students that they are not going to talk about how the character looks—*beautiful* won't even be on the word wall. The author has already described all of the characters. Instead, the students are to take the clues they have and use them to make judgments and draw conclusions about the characters. The words the teacher uses will name the skills students are being asked to practice—and they should be familiar to them because the teacher will have used these same words at this same point during the earlier modeling. The teacher has now given the students a focus for their reading—to decide what the main character is like as a person.

On Wednesday, students will be asked to make some connections, a key strategy in engaging students with texts. As they read today, they will be asked to think about the ways the main character is like them. This, too, will have been modeled earlier with a read aloud followed by a three-column chart, on which the teacher jotted down ways the character and the teacher were alike. The chart created in that lesson will be displayed, and the teacher will quickly remind students of the thinking that was modeled as the chart's columns were filled in: shared trait in the middle column and quick examples of that trait for the character on the left and the teacher on the right (Appendix F). The teacher's model will remain on the board as students read and as they complete their own notes.

On Thursday, students will be asked to consider how the character differs from themselves, this time using a T-chart (Appendix G). This, again, would have been modeled. The model will be reviewed and left up as a reference.

On Friday, the teacher will extend student thinking by asking students to think about *why* the author gave the main character the traits they've been describing. How did the type of person the main character is impact the other elements of the plot—the setting, the events, the other characters, the problem and its solution? Again, they will use a T-chart and short phrases to gather the information (Appendix H). This, too, will be review territory—it will have been discussed at length through read alouds, shared reading, and group work.

All through the week, the teacher will be monitoring student notes and conferencing with students who are still confused about the skill. If a student cannot do step one—collecting the clues—going to step two would be pointless. Although the majority of the class might be ready for the Tuesday notes, there will be a handful of students who still struggle with what they were asked to do on Monday. Teacher conferences will start with these students, reviewing what clues are and how to find them—and their responses will be the same ones they couldn't do correctly the day before. And it will stay that way until the teacher can see that these students truly understand author's clues to characters.

Does this make the teacher's job more complicated? Absolutely! That is why it is critical that good notes are taken on each student. If most students have shown that they understand by the end of the week, it will be time to move on to something else. But the students who still haven't gotten it cannot be abandoned. Their needs will be addressed in a reteaching group *outside* of independent reading time.

In a month or so, the teacher may do another series of responses on character analysis—as soon as the students who previously struggled seem ready. It will be an important skill sharpener for those who seem to understand and will give the formerly confused students a chance to show what they have learned.

Creating Responses

To create organized thinking responses, consider these things:

- How can you use your assigned responses to broaden your students' vision of the world of texts?
- What do your students need to be able to do to enjoy the texts they are reading?
- What is the skill that will help them develop this ability?
- What strategies support this skill?
- What expectations about the text do you have that help you exhibit this skill almost effortlessly?
- As a skilled reader, what steps do you take to successfully use this skill to help you engage with the texts you read—and in what order?
- What type of graphic organizer will best help your students organize the thinking required for this skill—a list, a T-chart, a Venn diagram, a chart, a web?
- Have you modeled all the steps you will ask your students to take and created charts they can use as models as they work independently on this skill or strategy?
- Have you made sure that every student has a text in which they can appropriately practice the targeted skills and strategies?
- Have you tried using this organizer with your own reading to be sure it shapes thinking in a way that will help your students grow as readers and does not, instead, get in the way?
- Can students complete the organizer in 5 minutes or less if they have understood both the text and the assignment?

- Will a quick review of this organizer help you separate the students who "get it" from those who don't?
- How will you vary your responses for these two groups of students?

Talk as a Response

Real-world readers talk about what they've read with other readers, so it is important that teachers carve out time for their students to do the same. At least once a week, students should gather the notes they have taken and meet with a partner or small group to talk about what they are reading. They can be directed to talk about specifics, such as character development, or generalities, such as what they like best about their books. It doesn't matter that they're all reading different books at different levels—they are all readers who have important things to say. These conversations, on which their teachers should gleefully eavesdrop, move students ever closer to becoming *readers* in the truest sense of the word.

A Brief Word about Accountability

In this era of accountability, teachers often seem to carry a huge weight on their shoulders, the weight of being certain all their students are able to pass their state's annual assessment. I teach in Texas—and currently, our third- and fifth graders *must* pass our state assessment to be promoted to the next grade. This is tremendously stressful for the students, their teachers, and their parents.

The skills tested on our state assessment are the same skills I use as a proficient and joyful reader to engage with the texts I read in my real life. They are also the skills I use to wade through my graduate-school textbooks. The state tests these skills because they are important.

If teachers are dedicated to the goal of creating true readers in their classrooms—readers who find so much joy in reading that they surround themselves with a variety of texts that they read for a variety of personally meaningful purposes—they will *want* their students to develop these skills and to know the strategies that will make them successful. They will look at their state and district curriculum with new eyes, seeing that the things for which the students are held accountable are important and worthy of their students' and their own time. But they must focus on helping the students develop these skills in authentic texts that they themselves have chosen.

Students should continually be pushed into higher levels of texts as they show they are ready. The should be armed with strategies to use to work through texts that are generally above their independent reading levels. Teachers must tell them always how what is being taught will help them as readers—*not* as test takers. The teacher's goal should not be to have students pass a test, but to help them learn to love reading. If that goal can be accomplished, the test will take care of itself.

References

Bear, D. R., Invernizzi, M., Templeton, S. R., & Johnston, F. (2003). *Words their way.* New York: Prentice Hall.

Harvey, S., & Goudvis, A. (2000). *Strategies that work.* York, ME: Stenhouse.

Keene, E. O., & Zimmermann, S. (1997). *Mosaic of thought: Teaching comprehension in a reader's workshop.* Portsmouth, NH: Heinemann.

Nixon, J. L. (1987). *A family apart.* New York: Bantam Doubleday Dell.

Probst, R. (1998). Reader–response theory in the middle school. In K. Beers & B. G. Samuels (Eds.), *Into focus* (pp. 125–138). Norwood, MA: Christopher-Gordon.

Rosenblatt, L. (1995). *Literature as exploration.* New York: Modern Language Association.

Routman, R. (2003). *Reading essentials.* Portsmouth, NH: Heinemann.

Chapter 5

Desksize Conferencing: A Launchpad for Growth

*M*uch to my amazement, Robert was actually reading that day—and had been reading every day that week. This was unusual behavior for him. He was repeating the grade and had always hated reading—independent reading time was usually the time he dreaded most in the day. But all this week, he had been engrossed in an *Animorphs* book. Or so I thought.

Robert's teacher, one of the most skilled I know, had spent most of the last week teaching inferring, and the students were to be keeping track of their inferences as they read. During my conferences, I was going to see how the students were doing with this important skill.

I pulled up a chair next to Robert and said, "So, you're reading *Animorphs*, huh? Are you enjoying it?"

"Yeah, it's okay."

"I see you're on page 87," I noted as I wrote the book title and page number on an address label headed with his name. "Tell me what's been happening so far."

Robert explained that "some guy" was underground running. "Have you made any inferences so far?"

"Not really."

"You don't have any thoughts on what's about to happen? You said he's running?"

"Yeah."

Clearly, we were getting nowhere, so I asked Robert to start reading to me. He was at a pivotal point in the plot when the protagonist was going to have to use his intelligence to help him escape. When Robert read that the hero felt a sharp tooth bite into his leg, I stopped him. "What do you think just happened?" I asked, trying to prompt an inference.

His eyes lit up. "A shark got him!" he exclaimed.

Not quite the answer I had in mind. Robert had just read 3 pages describing slithering creatures with sharp teeth that were chasing our brave hero through subway tunnels. The creatures' teeth had been described in horrifying detail. This should have been an easy inference to make. Where in the world did the sharks come from?

"Why do you think it's a shark?" I asked, as Robert happily began to jot down his truly amazing inference.

"Because sharks have sharp teeth and it says right here that he felt a sharp tooth in his leg. Must have been a shark."

Needless to say, I spent a while with Robert that day. I explained that inferences are a junction between what is in the text and what is in our heads—but they must always start with the text. This text contained no sharks.

"But what else could have bitten his leg?" Robert asked.

I went back and reread the pages describing the creatures that were emerging from deep in the subway tunnel to devour everything in their path. When I finished all the specific description of horrific teeth one more time, I said, "Now do you know what bit him?"

"No."

"Robert," I said, "I'm going to read this one more time, and I want you to use the words I read to make pictures in your head."

"What do you mean make pictures in my head?"

"You know, let the words help you call up images in your mind so you see what's happening in the book like a movie."

"You're kidding, aren't you?" he asked in amazement.

No, I most certainly was not. If I had waited to read Robert's page of inferences, I would never have realized that he not only did not understand that good inferences must be tied to information in the text, but that he also did not ever make pictures in his head. This is especially significant when a student is reading science fiction, a genre that presents creatures and inventions that we have never really seen. Without the ability to visualize, science fiction can be almost incomprehensible.

That day, Robert and I discussed three important things that he needed at exactly that moment: understanding the characteristics of the genre of science fiction, using words to make pictures in your head, and tying inferences to the text you are reading. Robert had been exposed to every idea we discussed multiple times in his school career and had not internalized any of it—but that day, he actually *needed* these ideas to comprehend. We had just shared a classic "teachable moment." Had I been sitting down reading or working with a small group while Robert grappled with his *Animorphs* books, he might still believe a subway shark had attacked our brave hero.

What Is Deskside Conferencing?

Deskside conferencing is a conversation between a teacher and a student that serves two purposes: It builds a relationship between the teacher and student, and it provides direction to help the student grow as a reader. These conferences are, in my opinion, the most important and effective teaching I do in the course of a day.

Deskside conferences are teacher initiated but student driven. They take place wherever students are reading—which may be on the floor or in the hallway rather than at a desk. Although teachers may plan a focus for the conferences before they begin them or plan what students they want to see that day, these plans are always subject to change—and change is the one constant during conferencing time.

Unlike the conferencing that occurs in lower grades that often focuses on issues of decoding and fluency (Calkins, 2001), conferences in the intermediate grades and higher focus on comprehension and strategy use. Yes, there are students whose decoding skills are far below where they should be at this level, but these needs, as well as the needs of fluency-challenged readers, should be addressed in guided reading groups.

The decoding work teachers do with students as they learn to read is much like the scales and simple melodies piano teachers require as students learn to play piano. The fingerwork and note reading that these early exercises require build the underlying structure for the later ability to play Debussy's *Clair de Lune*. The more students practice, the more advanced the music becomes, until finally, instead of playing one-note-at-a-time versions of classics, such as *Twinkle, Twinkle Little Star*, students are able to play *music*!! If students are taught to choose books at an appropriate level to read during independent reading time, they will be given a chance to move past exercises in decoding and to reach a point where the power of the words—not their discrete parts—will drive their reading.

It is important that when students are reading independently, they read in books that do *not* require them to continually face decoding challenges. With the wide variety of books available at the reading levels of even the lowest intermediate- and middle school students, it is possible for every student in the room to find a readable text whose original purpose was to involve readers in a good story or to help them learn about a topic of interest to them. It is critical that the main focus with independent readers be on comprehension.

Preparing for the Conference

Four things are needed to begin the conferences, three of which can be purchased at any office supply store: a clipboard, address labels or some other paper on which to take notes, and a pen or pencil. The fourth essential is a true desire to know students as readers coupled with a willingness to offer advice intended to help them grow.

Teachers should always plan to check with the students on the skills or strategies that have been targeted during instruction. Early in the year, the focus should be on engagement. Teachers should check with students while they're reading to be sure they are involved in the texts they have chosen. If teachers have taught a strategy, such as making connections, the conversation could start with asking students to show a place where they made a connection and explain that connection to the teacher. If the class has worked on a skill, such as character analysis, the conference could start with the teacher asking for a character sketch of the main character. If the students can easily answer the questions that are asked, they are clearly doing fine and don't need help that day, so the teacher can move on to the next reader. But these students cannot be abandoned—tomorrow might bring a true reading challenge for them. It is essential to touch base every few days even with the most capable readers—they aren't finished growing and they will need care and support as well.

What Kinds of Things Are Taught in a Deskside Conference?

Anything that has ever been taught standing in front of the room or leading a guided reading group is likely to come up in a deskside conference as well. But teachers will be surprised by the vast variety of experiences they will need to share as they work with readers far less skilled than they are—far more will be taught at student desks than ever thought possible.

Here are some of the things I've taught in deskside conferences in the past 2 weeks:

- how to tell if a book is part of a series
- why the beginning of a book is often confusing
- how to carry information in a chapter book from one chapter to the next
- how to identify words that will help you make pictures in your head
- what to do when you come to a word you don't know
- how questions drive a reader forward into the text
- how nonfiction reading differs from fiction reading
- why readers go back and reread
- how to preview a book
- why it's important to read books at the right level for your growth as a reader
- how characters' actions give us insight into what they will do later
- how to figure out who's talking when you're reading dialogue
- how to figure out what the main problem is in a novel
- what kinds of things to focus on in a fiction book
- using "I wonder if ..." and "I'll bet ..." as thinking starters for inferring
- the difference between exposition and rising action
- how to read a timeline
- how to read a cross-section diagram
- why it's important to finish books
- the location of the Ionian Sea

While I may have taught, or be planning to teach, many of these things during direct instruction, it is the presentation of the information at the exact time it is needed that makes this type of teaching successful. In an age when differentiated instruction is getting so much attention, deskside conferencing represents differentiation at its best.

One Reader at a Time

My doctor serves as my role model for an effective deskside conference. When she is in the exam room with me, she focuses every bit of her attention on my needs as her patient. She does not allow interruptions from phone calls or other patients—the time she spends with me is time spent listening to *me* and analyzing what *I* need to remain healthy. She asks carefully chosen questions that help her further understand my current health needs. The questions she asks, the medicines she prescribes, and the guidance she gives all come from her knowledge of medicine, a knowledge I do not share, and for which I depend on her. Her explanations of my medical needs always help me understand what has caused my current condition and what *I* must do to get better. She does this with all her patients, focusing her attention on them one patient at a time.

Once she has diagnosed the problem and done the things only she can do, such as write a prescription or order a test, the rest is up to me. If I follow her directions and my health improves, we have both done our parts. If I *don't* follow her advice and *don't* get better, I will have to return to her, and we will have to start again.

During supported independent reading, the classroom becomes a sort of reading clinic. The room is filled with readers who can benefit from an expert's advice. For some, it will be a "well reader" check up—the teacher will just be touching base to see that students are still reading well, pronouncing them healthy, and moving on. Others will need more prescriptive help.

Teachers should approach a deskside conference the same way doctors such as mine approach patients' visits with them. They should focus for a period of time on one reader and one reader only, analyzing that reader's needs at the moment and sifting through their bank of knowledge about reading to provide exactly the right "cure" for the problem of the moment. If they're lucky, the reader is sailing along just fine and needs only a quick check-up. But if a student *is* in need of intervention, the teacher should be able to prescribe the right cure if the right questions are asked and the student's response is quickly analyzed.

In the end, the teacher must understand that the ultimate responsibility for healthy reading rests on the shoulders of the readers themselves. They must realize when they need help, participate in the conversation as the teacher works to guide them, and do the things that only they can do to make their reading better. Just like doctors, teachers must use their knowledge of reading to know what problems readers might be experiencing at this point in their development and ask questions that will help them assess whether or not these problems exist for these students. If they do, the teacher must be prepared to offer a solution—a strategy that will help them further develop as healthy readers. The teacher must be sure the students understand what they are to do next—and then walk away and trust them to do it. Some of them will—and some of them won't. Teachers will see the ones who don't act on their suggestions far more often than those who do.

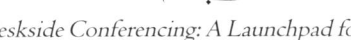

The Teacher's Deskside Manner

The Super Nanny was Oprah's guest on a recent show. Every time she gave a parent advice on dealing with an errant child, she advised, "Get down on the child's level and make direct eye contact. Use a steady and calm tone of voice." So, be advised by an expert and do the same—get down to the student's level, focus on that student, and use a calm and friendly tone of voice.

I conduct the majority of my conferences on my knees. To stand above a student while conferencing conveys a sense of control. There should be no control issue in a conference—it is simply a two-way conversation. The student and teacher need to be on equal footing so there is no power struggle involved.

The time spent conferencing with a student is sacred. During that slice of time, the teacher's attention should be on that student and that student only. With time, the other students will know, without doubt, that their turn with the teacher will come. They need to honor the time given to another member of the community.

The Purpose and Structure of a Conference

A deskside conference is a way of assessing the reading health of students in the classroom and providing targeted instruction at the point of need. It is a way of supporting students as they work in their individual zones of proximal development (Vygotsky, 1978). Its purpose is always to push students to greater levels of reading proficiency.

The conference generally has five parts:

- the initial question
- analysis of the student's response
- the focusing comment
- the guiding advice
- the check for understanding

Initiating the Conference

Conferences should begin with a question from the teacher to the student. The questions I use most often are:

- What are you reading today?
- Do you like your book so far?
- How's the reading going today?
- What's been happening, so far, in your book?
- What page are you on right now?

These simple questions are nonthreatening and open the door for further conversation. They temporarily take the reader's attention away from the text and focus it on what they are doing as readers.

These seemingly casual questions actually provide important information to the teacher. Students who often change books are asked what they are reading today, to see if they have finally found a book that engages them. If not, the work today will be on engagement. If students who have had trouble finding a book to enjoy are reading for the second or third day in the same book, asking what they like about the book, so far, will help the teacher know what kinds of books they are enjoying so they can be steered to their next good read. Asking how the reading is going today helps the teacher see if the teaching done previously helped the students or if students who have been reading right along have suddenly hit a snag, as can certainly happen in more sophisticated, longer texts. Students who have been having trouble comprehending or keeping a storyline in mind as they read through chapter books will be asked what's been happening in their book. Their answers will indicate if they need to go back and reread, or if they're doing quite well. And for readers who are lost in the world a book has created for them, as well as readers who are making such slow progress that the teacher suspects that they might be in a book that's over their heads, a good question to use is, "What page are you on right now?"

Tone of voice is everything. The teacher's inflection should never give students a clue as to why the questions is being asked. It is very tempting with students who have changed books five times in the last 6 days to say, "And what are you reading *today*?" but that clearly puts the student on the defensive from the beginning—and students won't learn if they are spending their time with an adversary for whom they feel they must provide a credible defense. In deskside conferencing, a supportive tone is everything.

Assessing the Responses

Once the initial question has been asked, the teacher must be prepared to listen carefully to students' answers and to hear the hidden problems they reveal. It is generally easy to tell when students' reading is going well—they see the interruption as just that and are obviously anxious to get back to what they were doing. But that doesn't mean the teacher shouldn't check to be sure these students are understanding the thinking they've been asked to do to complete the day's response. Once the teacher has established that they are, in fact, on track, they should be left alone to return to the books they are enjoying.

But most of the students will need more attention than that. Some will be struggling with finding books they enjoy; some will be steadfastly returning to books that are comfortable but not at a challenging enough reading level for them; some will be having trouble figuring out what is happening in the text they're reading; some will be confused about how to read a genre that may be new to them. With every reader every day, the teacher must *expect* to uncover confusion—and be prepared to offer some advice to minimize it.

In the seconds after the students respond to the initial question, the teacher must quickly decide on what the focus will be for the conference that day. Often, teachers will have an idea in mind before stopping at the student's desk because they will have reviewed their previous notes and have an idea where that student may be struggling. Sometimes, they will plan to spend the day assessing individual students' understanding of the important skills or strategies they have been so madly teaching during direct instruction and shared and guided reading. But in the end, it will be each student's response to the very first questions that sets the direction—and the length—of the conference.

Sharpening the Focus of the Conference and Offering Advice That Guides

I remember the first time I ever used a microscope. We were looking at drops of pond water to see, in magnified horror, all the tiny creatures that inhabit that universe—and my partner was oohing and aahing. I couldn't wait for my turn!

But when my turn came, I couldn't see a thing. I just couldn't get the hang of looking with one eye and focusing the scope so I could actually see. What a disappointment—the rest of my sixth-grade class now realized whose territory we were invading each time we swam in a pond—but my lack of focus kept me in the dark.

Students' vision of reading shouldn't be blurred. For a conference to be successful, it is not enough for *teachers* to understand what they are hoping to accomplish that day. It needs to be a shared vision that both the student and teacher agree will be beneficial for that reader that day. If only *the teacher's* focus is clear, the conference will be a failure.

Once the focus for the intervention has been determined, teachers must clearly state that focus to the student. Teachers need to name the problem they've detected and what type of advice they plan to offer. Teachers also have to remember that students bring strengths to their reading every day—and they will develop more quickly if the tools they have already mastered are continually celebrated.

For students who are having trouble finding books that capture their attention, the effort they've made in choosing the book they're holding should always be honored. If their response to a question about enjoying the book they have is lukewarm or negative, the teacher might say, "I see you've picked an adventure book. Those books are always fun to read. Let's talk about what you can expect to find at the beginning of an adventure book." This honors the student's choice, makes an assumption about why engagement may not have occurred as yet, and stated what help the teacher is planning to offer that day.

For students who are continuing to read comfortable texts, it is good to cut a deal. After asking what they're reading today, the teacher might say, "You have really been enjoying these *Amber Brown* books. I think you've read about three of them so far, haven't you? I really like them, too—because Amber is *funny*! I don't want you to give up reading these books, but I'd like you to try reading some at a little bit higher level. You've improved so much as a reader, that I think you're ready to try something different. Why don't you go ahead and finish this *Amber Brown*, and I'll get some *Melanie Martin* and *Ramona Quimby* books for you to choose from for your next read? I think you'll like them—and I'll help you get started in one when the time comes." The problem has been named—the book is not challenging enough—but the student's right to choose has been honored, and she has been allowed to finish a book she will most likely enjoy. The teacher has complimented her growth as a reader—and made a plan for what to read next. The teacher must honor the promise and bring in some books from which she can choose. In addition, the teacher must expect the student to honor her promise as well. She will need to actually read the book she chooses. The teacher must be certain that any book offered will be one the student is capable of reading—with support.

If a student's answer to "What's happening in your book so far?" is vague or clearly confused, the teacher might say, "Why don't you read a little bit of the book to me?" The teacher will be listening to see if the book is actually above the student's level and too much time is being spent dealing with unfamiliar words and sentence structures. If that is the case, the teacher could say, "Boy, you really seem to be fighting with this text—that can't be much fun. Would you like to find another book that you might enjoy more? It's important to enjoy the time we spend reading." Then, the student will be asked what needs to be considered when the next book is chosen and then be sent to the school or classroom library or offered a stack of texts at the correct level for him to look through. The teacher should allow him to abandon the book because students should never hate the time they spend reading.

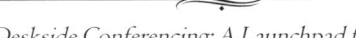

Sometimes, asking students to just go back to the last point at which they understood what was going on is enough support, even if they go all the way back to page one. When asking students to find the last place where they were sure what was going on, teachers should always ask them to summarize what happened up to that point and to read a page or two aloud. The teacher should listen carefully to the text and help the students notice the important information the author provided for the reader. If students don't seem to understand how the teacher knew that would be important, it is important to explain that readers should go into fiction *expecting* to find out things about the setting, the characters, their problems, and the solutions or into nonfiction *expecting* to learn something new. Readers must look for these things because no one can find what they're not looking for. Often, this is enough to get a student going—but the teacher will need to check back with the student every single day for a week or more to be certain that the text is manageable.

Some of the issues to consider when focusing a conference are:

- Has the student changed books? If so, ask why.
- If the student has chosen to abandon a book, what mistakes were made in choosing the book? The teacher needs to help the student think about the choice and plan what to do differently next time.
- Is the student making steady progress through the book? If not, the teacher needs to take the time to determine if the book is comprehensible for, and interesting to, the student.
- Can the student summarize what has happened, so far, in the book? If not, the teacher needs to determine if the book is at too high a level or if the student is only going through the motions of reading and respond accordingly.
- What challenges does the book present—subplots, playing with time, suspension of belief, etc.? Is the student aware of these challenges and sophisticated enough to cope with them? If not, the teacher will need to offer support meant to help the student meet these challenges.

- Does the student know how to carry information across from one chapter and one day to the next? If not, the teacher should offer a graphic organizer that may help.

- Does the student know on what to focus attention while reading—characters setting, events, problem, and solution for fiction; new learning, main ideas, and details for nonfiction? If not, the teacher should reteach this at the desk and offer a graphic organizer to help guide thinking.

- Is the student able to apply the strategies taught in the classroom to the text currently being read? If not, the teacher should model a strategy using the student-selected text and then ask the student to do the same, being sure the student understands what to do.

- Is the student able to exhibit the skills taught in the classroom and tested on the state assessment in the text currently being read? If not, the teacher should try to determine if the problem is the application of the skill or the level of the text and respond accordingly.

- Is the student reading from a wide variety of texts? If not, the teacher should help to broaden the student's reading tastes by discussing other genres that might be considered and offering to help the student select a book in that genre and begin to read it.

- Does the student understand the structure of the text being read? If not, the teacher should review how to determine text structure and offer a graphic organizer to help organize thinking.

- Is the student reading at a level that will promote growth? If the book is too easy, the teacher should help guide the reader to a more challenging text. If the book is too hard, the teacher should see if the student could actually read it with more support or if another choice needs to be made.

- Can the reader articulate what he or she likes about the book currently being read? If not, the teacher should try to determine if the problem is that the book is not being understood or that the student is not engaged in that book.

- How did the student choose the book currently being read? If the book is not a good choice, the teacher should review previewing a book and using the five-finger rule.

- Can the reader describe the main character in a fiction book? If not, the teacher should review character clues and model how to find and

use these clues using the student-selected text, then ask the student to do the same while the teacher watches.
- Does the reader understand the graphics and other features of nonfiction texts? If not, the teacher should take the time to review this using the features in the student-selected text.
- Does the reader understand that many nonfiction books do not have to be read straight through? If not, the teacher should remind the student and talk about how to use that knowledge as a reader.
- Would reading *with* the student for a few pages help the student become more interested in the text? If so, the teacher should take the time to do just that, sharing the thinking as they read.
- Does the student need to go back and reread to clear up confusions? If so, the teacher should help the student locate the place where meaning broke down and stay with the student as he or she begins to reread and repair understanding.
- What questions does the student have about the book currently being read? Is the student even able to articulate any confusions? If not, the teacher should take the time to let the student understand that readers always have questions while reading—some drive the reading forward and others force the reader to go back and reread or to think harder about the text.
- Does the reader understand the response graphic that has been assigned? If not, the teacher should reteach it at the desk and listen to the student talk through a possible response.

Checking for Understanding

Teachers should never leave a student's side until they are confident that that reader understands what to do next. They should restate what they've asked the student to do and usually end with, "Do you think that will help?" If the student is not convinced that the advice and guidance offered will help him or her as a reader, the teacher has just wasted everyone's time.

Students must find what the teacher has asked them to do valuable—or they will never do it. They must also believe that they are capable of being competent readers. Jensen (1998) points out that a feeling of personal control over a situation is essential for remediating or preventing learned helplessness, a condition he describes as being characterized by "nearly complete apathy and persistent passivity" (p. 57). If the goal is to develop a lifelong love of reading in students, teachers have a professional responsibility to challenge developing readers' views of themselves as incompetent. They must learn to share the belief that they can comprehend and enjoy texts.

Knowing the Readers through Conferencing

The most important benefit of deskside conferencing is that it is through these informal conversations at students' desks that teachers learn to truly know their students as readers. They will know their reading tastes, their reading strengths, their reading challenges. By meeting regularly one-on-one with every student, teachers become acutely aware of what their groups' needs are. The information gathered from these conferences should drive direct instruction, as well as shared and guided reading.

Deskside conferences help students become better readers—but even more importantly, they help teachers become better at teaching reading. More can be learned about reading through these conversations with developing readers than any book could ever teach. Every day, students will learn what types of books they love and what sorts of challenges they face in trying to read them.

By listening to students and working with them to help overcome any obstacles that keep them from truly loving the time they spend reading, teachers can be reminded every day that there is a deep need in all of us to be good at the things that are important. Reading is important—and no matter how much the students in any classroom try to deny it, they are deeply aware of its value. They want to be good readers—and their teachers should want that for them. Deskside conferences are a powerful way of helping them reach that goal—one day, one student, and one conquered obstacle at a time.

References

Calkins, L. M. (2001). *The art of teaching reading.* New York: Addison-Wesley.

Jensen, E. (1998). *Teaching with the brain in mind.* Alexandra, VA: Association for Supervision and Curriculum Development.

Vygotsky, L. S. (1978). *Mind in society: The development of higher psychological processes.* Cambridge, MA: Harvard University Press.

Trade Books Cited

Applegate, K. The *Animorphs* series. New York: Scholastic.
Cleary, B. The *Ramona Quimby* series. New York: HarperCollins.
Danziger, P. The *Amber Brown* series. New York: Scholastic.
Weston, C. The *Melanie Martin* series. New York: Dell Yearling.

Chapter 6

Conferencing with Delayed Readers

*S*truggling reader. This is the term reading teachers use as a catch-all phrase to describe all the students in their classrooms who aren't making the progress they had hoped.

But the term *struggling* is a misnomer. According to *Webster's New World College Dictionary, Fourth Edition* (2002), to *struggle* is to "make great efforts or attempts; strive; labor." This would imply that these students are valiantly fighting to conquer the skill of reading. In truth, their *teachers* are laboring with great and continued effort, but many of the students themselves usually have quit "struggling" ages ago. Like the adventurer trapped in quicksand, they have quit fighting it; they are floating on their backs, accepting their fate, and waiting for someone to rescue them.

Webster's defines the word *delay*, however, as "to put off to a future time; postpone." If a plane flight is *delayed*, it will, in fact, arrive eventually and the passengers will, indeed, reach their destination. They won't get there when they were expected, but they will achieve their goal of traveling from Point A to Point B.

Below-level readers can be seen in this same light. They are not struggling; they are delayed. They have not developed reading skills and proficiencies on the planned schedule, but they are capable of catching up. They will need to be carefully assessed to determine the reasons for their delay and then provided with opportunities to strengthen the reading muscles they will need to catch up. It means they will need more focused attention than some of the other readers in the room who are sailing along at the expected speed—and they will definitely need to consume words at a rate far above what they have done in the past. But it does *not* sentence them to a lifetime of below-level reading performance.

Understanding the Delayed Reader

Last week, the fifth graders' scores on Texas's high-stakes assessment arrived at campuses across the state. "High stakes" is an understatement in this case; the students must pass this test to be promoted to sixth grade. They have taken it once, and if they fail it, they are in for 5 weeks of intense interventions aimed at helping them pass it the second time it is given in April. If they fail it again, they will be required to go to summer school and take the test a third time in July. Those who still do not pass will repeat fifth grade next year.

I was curious about the academic histories of the students from my building who had failed this test, so my math partner and I went to the registrar's office and began going through the students' permanent records. The vast majority of the students who had failed this test have struggled with reading (and often, academics in general) since first grade. Many of them have been "placed" in the next grade every year, even though they were not performing at the expected levels in their subjects. Since our state also requires the passing of the third-grade state test, we discovered that many of these students failed *that* test the first time through and often didn't pass it until the third administration, then passing it only by a hair. These students have been challenged readers for a long time.

Research has given us valuable insights into the workings of the human brain. One body of research with immense implications for delayed readers is the research into emotions, particularly the brain's reactions to a perceived threat. When the brain perceives that a person is threatened in some way, it immediately kicks into the "fight or flight" mode, operating purely on emotion for the moment. Once the brain takes a closer look at the stimulus and determines it is not, in fact, a threat, emotions calm down and the individual is able to respond more rationally. But what if the brain determines that person *is* being threatened? What happens then?

LeDoux (1996) cites various studies that show that emotion overrides thinking when people are threatened. At this point, in fact, people revert to survival mode in what Caine and Caine (1994) call downshifting and Goldman (1995) calls an emotional hijacking. Once individuals feel threatened, they can see only two choices—fighting the thing that threatens them or running from it.

This is the situation that intermediate- and middle school delayed readers must encounter every day. They are continually asked to perform tasks for which they are not yet fully equipped, not just in reading class, but in science and social studies as well. Even math requires reading abilities. They know they've never been good at reading—the neon lights of failed tests and failed subjects have flashed in their faces for as long as they can remember. And they are still children, no matter how mature their bodies may appear. Brain research shows that heir frontal cortex has not yet developed to the point where they can rationally think their way through challenges (Brownlee, 1999). They respond in a purely human manner—they either flee from reading by pretending to do it or they fight their inadequacies by continuing to try to read books they don't understand or by acting out in class. Their continued inability to engage with texts leaves them farther and farther behind the students who are actually making expected progress—and the level of the threat increases as time goes on.

The Behaviors of Delayed Readers

By the intermediate grades, delayed readers basically fall into two categories: those who are still trying and those who have already given up. By middle school, almost all of these challenged readers fall into the latter category and aren't even pretending they care about reading. Whether they're receptive or hostile, the teachers' job as their guide is to spend enough individual time with these readers to begin to understand what is blocking their reading progress and to then offer focused support to engage them with texts, improve their skills, and lead to them to a lifelong love of reading.

Some delayed readers are easier to identify than others. They are the ones who command their teachers' attention whether they are ready to give it to them or not. In an effort to fight against reading, they never have a book at their desks ready to read. They don't get out their reading logs or response journals—and they dare their teachers to notice and correct their behavior. Some of them refuse to read at all unless the teacher personally sits with them and gets them started—and then they quit the minute their teacher walks away.

Others are more compliant and would probably be overlooked in a classroom where the teacher was not actively involved in conferencing during independent reading time. These are the students who dutifully open their books, log them in, and attempt to read them. Some will appear to be doing fine, not even their expressions hinting to the fact that they are not understanding a thing they are reading. Others will wear the look of a person straining to accomplish a difficult task, brows furrowed with concentration and bodies tensed. But their brains, keenly aware of the threat posed by this task they are ill-equipped to complete, will not be functioning in a way that leads to actual understanding.

Reducing the Threat of Reading

Sylwester (1995) cites a 1984 study by Maddi and Kobasa that looked at the ability of executives to deal with high levels of stress. Their study determined that those who thrived under stressful conditions shared three important qualities: an understanding that challenges are necessary for growth, a strong commitment to important people in their lives, and a belief that they themselves control the solutions to any problems that might come their way. This research can guide teachers as they work with delayed readers who must manage the stress of being asked to read when they believe they are incompetent at doing so. If teachers can help them see reading as a manageable challenge rather than a threat, provide them with opportunities to prove to themselves that they can solve their problems independently, and offer them focused support and encouragement that will create a committed bond between student and teacher, tremendous gains will result as these students grow not just as readers, but as self-directed learners as well.

Supported independent reading embraces the ideas of challenge, commitment, and control. By helping readers learn to choose books at a level that will challenge but not frustrate them, by giving them control over their reading and offering hints that will help them learn to overcome obstacles on their own, and by modeling their own commitment to these students as unique individuals so that a bond is established that is directed toward success, their teachers are helping them reframe their expectations for reading. Instead of expecting to be frustrated by the reading experience, they will learn to expect to be challenged so that they can grow. When teachers have changed the expectations, they have changed the readers—and miraculous growth can then occur.

Conferencing with a Helpless Reader

Helpless readers are readers who don't think they can possibly read a book without teachers by their sides. They have usually been identified early on as a "struggling reader," and, with all the best intentions, have had books carefully chosen for them and been guided through every text in a guided reading group. They are often eager to please the teacher—they just have never learned that they can also please themselves. The focus for these conferences is always on building confidence and filling the readers' toolboxes with what they need to work through increasingly more complex texts.

Kendra is a helpless reader. The minute I walk into her classroom each day, her song begins, "Mrs. Allison, will you read with me today?" If I tell her I have to start my conferences today with some other reader, she will pout and refuse to read or she will try to interrupt the conference to tell me what page she is on. Unless I am sitting with *her,* her behavior often needs to be addressed and redirected. She has such a cemented view of herself as an incapable reader, that when I complimented her one day on the unbelievable progress she was truly making, she spent the next week on a crusade to prove me wrong, refusing to read and declaring that any book she had in her hand was too hard for her. She just could not accept the fact that she was starting to become a reader capable of reading alone.

To helpless readers, those are fighting words—they are so convinced that their efforts will end in failure that a recent record of success puts them in a state of confusion. And when someone points out that they've been successful of late, they seem determined to prove that all their success has been a fluke. Instead of choosing to succeed, they fall back into a cycle of failure—unless a teacher catches them midfall and puts their feet back on the path to success.

Kendra can read a *Junie B. Jones* book in two sittings—and that is exactly what she wants to do. In fact, she'd really rather read a picture book that she can finish in a matter of minutes. Earlier in the year, I had helped her through her first *Amber Brown* book, and then those became her passion. But when she started to be able to finish those books quickly as well, I wanted her to start reading at the next higher level and showed her several *Melanie Martin* books, explaining that she could only continue to grow as a reader if she continued to challenge herself.

Initially, Kendra was so excited about *Melanie Martin* books that she chose two at the library and smiled ear to ear as she told me about her dilemma in trying to decide which one to read first. Many of the other girls in the class had been tearing through this particular series and had told her how good the books were. She finally chose *The Diary of Melanie Martin or How I Survived Matt the Brat, Michelangelo, and the Leaning Tower of Pizza* (Weston, 2000) and began to read. But this book was at a higher reading level than the books she'd been enjoying, though still well within her now-higher reading range—and when she hit her first confusion—Melanie's use of italicized Italian words followed by parenthesized pronunciations—Kendra gave up and decided she didn't like the book.

"I don't like this book," she pouted at the beginning of our conference. "It's stupid."

"What don't you like about it?" I asked.

"I just told you," she said. "It's stupid."

I tried to probe further. "Help me understand what makes the book stupid," I suggested.

"Everything," she replied.

Seeing that this line of questioning was going nowhere, I suggested that we read together and asked her to start. We weren't three lines down in the book before she hit the first Italian word and quit reading.

I pronounced the word for her and showed her how the italics identified the foreign words and that the parenthetical information right after it was Melanie's way of showing how to pronounce it. "These are Italian words," I said. "Even the author doesn't expect you to know them—that's why she gave you this information on how to pronounce them."

"I don't want to read any Italian words!" Kendra insisted. "They're stupid. I want to get another book."

I truly believed that Kendra could read the book she had chosen—but she had clearly decided otherwise. No matter how often I checked in with her, she continued to fight reading the book.

I was so determined that Kendra needed to read this book to prove to herself that she could do it that I wouldn't even let her turn it in at the library. I had her classroom teacher and the librarian both on full alert—that book was *not* to be turned in. It became a running joke between Kendra and me. Her eyes would twinkle and she'd look at me and say, "I turned in that *Melanie* book, Mrs. Allison." She'd even stop me in the hall to tease me about it. But I stubbornly marched ahead, determined that I would get her through that book. I believed that by finishing that book she would prove to herself that she was capable of reading on a higher level. This was a strategy that had previously worked with many other readers.

One deal I cut with her was that she could read some other book every other day—after all, true readers read more than one book at a time. She usually chose picture books—we were back to wanting to finish a book in a sitting. On the days she was tackling her *Melanie Martin* book, I kept telling her, "Just read to page 25 and then we'll talk." She'd hit page 25—and still proclaim that the book was stupid. Then it was page 36, and finally page 50—every page a battle of wills between her and me. Finally, I threw in the towel and personally walked her to the library to drop the "stupid" book in the book drop.

"Kendra," I began, "thank you for really giving this book a good try. You've read to page 50 and still don't like the book. Everybody picks the wrong book sometimes, and it certainly isn't any fun to read if you're not enjoying the book you're in. I really don't want you reading something you are not enjoying, so let's think about what was wrong with this book and then go to the library together to find one you'll like better."

Kendra decided that the main problem was that she had only looked at the back of the book and not at any of the pages, so she didn't know it would be written with Italian words. She decided she needed to be sure and do the five-finger rule on at least two pages of a book before she chose one.

She wanted a Dan Gutman book that another student had read, and I commented on the fact that readers get ideas from other readers all the time. When we couldn't find that particular book, she settled on a *Bailey School Kids* book and checked a couple of the pages before checking it out. She read it without my help in 4 days, completely engaged each day, and moved on to another book in that series. She believes she won this battle—she didn't have to read her *Melanie* book. The real victory, however, is that she found a book she truly enjoyed reading. My guidance for her now will continue to be to choose progressively more difficult books, so she will continue to grow.

I am aware that the *Bailey Street Kids* book, slightly below the lowest end of Kendra's zone of proximal development (ZPD), is an easier read than the *Melanie Martin* book, which was near the high end of her ZPD. But her attitude toward reading is far more important than the reading level of the book.

Giving the control back to Kendra as the reader made all the difference. To take control of reading choices away from helpless readers, no matter how well intentioned, moves them farther away from, not closer to, true independence. After reading at this comfortable level for a week or two, it will be time again to push her to harder reading, this time at more of a midpoint in her reading zone.

When working with helpless readers, the main priorities should be building reader self-confidence and helping these readers learn to take control of their own reading. Series books are usually a good scaffold for these students as they learn to read for enjoyment and begin to expect to understand what they read. Carlsen (1994) reminds us that these books provide what he terms "unconscious delight" and are the first of several predictable phases that lead to a lifelong love of reading. Although students who are making the expected progress usually pass through the stage of unconscious delight much earlier in their academic careers, it is never too late to use the predictability of series books to teach the invaluable lesson that reading can, in fact, be fun.

A Conference with a Smoke and Mirrors Reader

Smoke and mirrors readers are accidental magicians—they can make the illusion of their reading seem real to the only people for whom they read—their teachers. In fact, they are so skilled at illusion that they often even fool themselves.

According to their reading logs, these students are making steady progress through the books they have chosen. Their behavior never needs redirection, and they will always say they are doing fine. They are the compliant students who do everything they are asked; the teacher has asked them to read, so they "read." But a quick look at their response graphics will show that there is a disconnect between what has been taught and what they have learned. And they aren't even aware that there's a problem. These readers are not trying to mislead anyone; they really believe they are doing fine. It is only through conferencing that their confusions can be uncovered so that they can learn to truly love reading.

Most smoke and mirrors readers do not seem to grasp the skills and strategies that capable readers use to make their way meaningfully through texts. The focus in these conferences should be on a clearer understanding of the skills and strategies that these readers do not yet own and on the importance of reading for their own pleasure, rather than just for pleasing someone else.

Maria is a smoke and mirrors reader. There is not a sweeter child in the entire classroom. She greets me with a smile every day, always wants a quick hug, and has not been off-task for one second of the entire school year. She logs in on her reading log, she reads the entire 30 minutes each day, and she always completes her response graphic without being told. But those responses tell the story—Maria is just not getting it.

This particular day, Maria was reading *Ramona the Pest* (Cleary, 1968). She was even smiling as she read, seemingly enjoying every word Beverly Cleary had set down on the page. I pulled up next to her and said, "You're smiling, Maria! You must really be enjoying this book."

"I am, Mrs. Allison," she said. "It's a really good book."

"Can you tell me what's been happening so far?"

"Well, Ramona is having a party and she's inviting a bunch of kids from her class."

"Sounds interesting. Have you made any inferences while you were reading?"

"Oh, yeah," she nodded, still smiling. "I've made a lot already."

"Great!" I said. "Could you share one with me?"

Conferencing with Delayed Readers

"Well, right here it says that Ramona's mom said she could have a party. That's what the text says. So I know that when moms say you can have a party, you can have a party. So my inference is that she's going to have a party."

Obviously, there's a party in Ramona's future—but just as obviously, Maria is totally off course on what it means to make an inference. She has part of the formula down—an inference is putting something from the text with something in your head. The part she *doesn't* get is that this mixture of information is supposed to result in a new idea that isn't anywhere on the page.

"Wow!" I said, stalling for time. "I can tell that you understand that to make an inference you have to combine the words on the page with something you know in your head. Let me see the inferences you made yesterday."

Just as I suspected, every inference she had made—and she had filled a page with them—took something on the page and basically restated it two more times, once in the column where she was to put what prior knowledge she had used and once more in the column for the actual inference.

Checking these graphics at student desks is often the best way to assess their thinking. If the students are required to have their reading logs and response graphics on the corner of their desks during reading time, the teacher can easily pick them up and check them. If this response had shown up on a stack of papers taken home for grading, the teacher might think the student was just being lazy and going through the motions. By asking Maria to show me her responses and talk me through them, I understood that she thought she was making true inferences. The problem wasn't lack of effort—it was lack of understanding.

"Maria," I said. "I think there's an important piece of inferring that you may not have understood when we talked about it in class—and that is my fault, not yours. Did you realize that an inference is something that is never actually written in the book? It is an idea the author wants you to make all on your own from the clues she gives you in the text. Your job as a reader is to find the clues, put them together with things you know in your head, and figure out what the author is trying to tell you."

Maria gave me a blank stare, obviously saddened by her perception that she had disappointed me. Pleasing her teachers is what Maria does best—and letting her continue to believe that she had failed in that goal would have weakened her self-image. In the process, a seed might have been planted that would grow into a strong belief that she was incompetent as a reader. This is too much damage to inflict on one child in one conference. With smoke and mirrors readers, teachers must always be aware that their acceptance of the student, warts and all, is the essential ingredient for that student's growth.

"Maria, inferring is one of the very hardest things to learn. That's why we start on it early in the year and work on it all the time—practice makes perfect! I *expect* everyone to make mistakes on their inferences. Mistakes show me where your thinking is confused, so that I can help you learn to straighten out that confused thinking. Every single person in this room is having trouble with inferences. You're learning to think like sophisticated readers—and you're bound to make some mistakes along the way. That's why I'm here. If you could do all this perfectly already, I'd be out of a job!"

Maria smiled shyly—and again looked me straight in the eye. "You are on the right track," I said, smiling back. "Let's talk about where your thinking derailed a bit and see if we can get you on your way. Let's go back to the beginning of this chapter and start looking for the clues the author has left us to trigger an inference."

Maria returned to the first page of the chapter and began reading. In this particular book, Ramona is captivated by a girl named Susan's curly hair. Cleary describes Susan's hair and Ramona's curiosity about whether or not those curls would spring back if they were touched. After Maria read this passage, I stopped her.

"In a book," I began, "everything is there for a reason. The author only puts things in a book that will be important later. Beverly Cleary has spent an awful lot of time right here talking about Susan and her curly hair—and how jealous Ramona is of that hair. You've read a Ramona book before. What do you know about Ramona?"

"She gets in lots of trouble doing things she shouldn't."

"Yes, she does. Does she do mean things?"

"No, she is just kind of interested in things and wants to see what will happen."

"You are so right," I said. "So, since she's so interested in Susan's curly hair and wants to see it spring back, what do you think will happen later in the book?"

"She might pull Susan's hair?" Maria guessed.

"*That*," I smiled, "is an inference! Is there any place on this page where it says that Ramona is planning to pull Susan's hair?"

"No," Maria responded.

"So, how did you figure that out?"

"I thought about what Ramona usually does and figured that that is why there was so much stuff about Susan's curly hair. It just seems like something Ramona would do."

"See there?" I grinned. "You *do* know how to make inferences! Let's see if we can figure out which column on your chart to put each of those ideas in."

I made sure that Maria understood that one column of her chart was for information that the author actually gave us, and one was for what she knew in her head that helped lead her to the third column, which was the inference itself.

"Now, can you see the difference between what you just did and the inferences you made yesterday?"

"I think so," she said, obviously not 100% sure.

"Okay, talk me through it," I prompted.

"Yesterday, I just kept putting stuff down that was already in the book. This time, I figured something out that wasn't written down already."

"*Bingo!*" I acknowledged. "What a great job you've done today. I'm going to go conference with some other people right now, but I'll check back in with you at the end of reading time to see if you've made another inference on your own. Remember that everything in a book is there for a reason and that part of the fun of reading is figuring out why the author put it there. When you do that, you are inferring."

Several things were done in this conference. The things Maria *did* understand about inferring were affirmed—that inferences always start with the words on the page and join that information to something the reader already knows. The point of the reader's confusion was explicitly named—that she didn't understand that an inference is something that is never written in the book itself. Her thinking was guided as she made an inference on her own through pointing out that what she knew about the character from reading other *Ramona* books is the type of prior knowledge that will lead to inferences. The reader then had to show that she understood how to use the graphic as a record of her thinking. The conference ended with asking the reader to explicitly explain what she did differently to make the inference she made with support. It was then made clear that she would be trusted to work on her own with this new understanding—but that her work would be checked later on to be sure she was clear on the day's conference focus.

Maria still struggles with inferring, but at least half of her inferences now are right on the mark. She still gets confused and still needs guidance and support, but she gets stronger every day and continues to work very hard. My conferences with her always have two goals—to clarify any confusions she has about the assignments that have been given and to help her start to develop a vision of herself as a competent reader who reads for her own pleasure rather than to please a teacher.

A Conference with a Starving Reader

Starving readers really want to read. They look at other students in the room who seem lost in the books they have chosen and want desperately to find that same type of pleasure in texts. They are hungry for guidance that will lead them to success—and they hang on every word that the teacher utters. In a conference with a starving reader, my focus is on the basic strategies that skilled readers use to understand what they are reading.

Amir is a starving reader. He has three older sisters, all of whom are avid readers. He is never without a book and always eager to start independent reading time. His enthusiasm is obvious—he can't wait to read. He always expects to enjoy what he is reading. There is only one problem—he often catches only part of what is going on in his books, and so, wanders through most of the text in a huge fog.

Everyone has driven in fog and made it safely to their destinations—but much of the scenery along the way was missed, which is particularly disappointing if the view was the reason for the trip in the first place. That is how Amir reads. He spends so much time just trying to stay on the road, focusing on decoding and making it to the next sentence, picking up just enough meaning to keep him headed in the right direction. But along the way, he misses so much of what the author has put there to help him enjoy his journey—and he does realize—and regret—that he is missing all that scenery. The conference's focus, then, should be on helping him learn how to clear away the fog.

This particular day, Amir is reading a *Geronimo Stilton* book. This series is cleverly designed, a great mixture of texts, graphics, and color that is pleasing to the eye. "What are you reading today?" I ask. "It looks really interesting."

Amir shows me the cover of his book. He does not tell me the title or even say that it is a *Geronimo Stilton* book—just showing me the cover seems to be enough. But he's smiling as he shows me.

"It's a good book, Mrs. Allison."

"It looks like a good book, Amir. What is it about?"

"This mouse wants to go to Egypt, but then he decides not to go."

I was fairly certain that Amir had missed something along the way. "I've never seen one of these books before, Amir," I began. "Do you mind if I look at it?"

I picked up the book and read the summary on the back, which explained that poor, overworked Geronimo kept planning vacations and then emergencies at work would make him miss his plane. This certainly was not Amir's take on the story.

Every starving reader with whom I've ever worked is truly grateful for guidance—they just aren't aware that they need it. I chose my words carefully for my conference with Amir.

"Amir, you are on the right track. Geronimo *did* plan to go to Egypt—but I think you missed something important about why he didn't go. Would you mind if we go back and reread that part?"

"That'd be great, Mrs. Allison," Amir smiled, obviously relieved.

I had to decide the best focus for learning for Amir. Since his teacher had been working on plot structure with the class, I decided to see if he understood what kinds of information are given in the beginning of a book.

I pointed to the "plot mountain" poster (Appendix I) that his teacher had posted in the front of the room. "Remember when Ms. V drew that mountain and explained to you how authors plan stories?" I asked.

"Yea," Amir grinned.

"Can you explain that to me, Amir?" I asked.

He sat and thought a minute, very eager to please me by knowing exactly what to say. Finally, he admitted, "I'm not really sure I understand that part, Mrs. Allison."

So, I began to reteach, hoping to start from a point that was clear to him. "Okay, Amir," I began, "when we read a story, what are the five important parts?"

"Character, setting, events, problem, and solution," Amir rattled off. "I remember that because of that sentence, *Cinderella saw every pretty star.*"

"That is great, Amir," I smiled. "Now, let's think about what the author does with those five elements at the beginning of a story.

"When an author starts a story, he starts here on the flat ground," I said, drawing a plot mountain on a sheet of paper and pointing to the left side of the chart. "We come into the story not knowing anything. We don't know any characters' names or if the story will take place in Texas or at the North Pole! We don't even know what the problem will be yet. We can get some of this information from the summary on the back of the book—but that won't give us all the information we need. We need to *expect* to find out all this stuff as we begin to read—we should be *looking* for information about the character, the setting, and the problem right from the beginning."

With that information in mind, Amir and I started again from the beginning. His instructions were to stop me every single time he learned something new about the character, the setting, or the problem. The book opened with Geronimo complaining how hot it was that August—and I stopped Amir. "What did you just learn?" I asked.

"He's hot," Amir said.

"Why is it so hot?" I asked.

He was obviously stumped. "Reread that last sentence," I said, "and listen for the information about what time of year it is."

As soon as he read the word *August,* a light went on for Amir. "It's *August!*" he screeched. "That's why it was so hot!"

"Exactly!" I smiled. "*That* is some good reading! Do you think that maybe you missed some other things here at the beginning that might be important?"

Amir is always honest—because he always truly wants to learn. "Yeah," he said, "I think I did."

"Okay, let's think of a way to help you catch all those details you missed the first time through. Do you think an organizer would help?"

"Yeah, it might," he said.

I asked if I could borrow a sheet of paper and then wrote C, S, P down the side—for characters, setting, and problem—leaving plenty of space to fill in information for each one. "These are the important things you have to figure out at the beginning of the book. Every time you learn something new about one of these things today, I want you to quickly write them down here—just enough words to help you remember. I'll check back with you at the end of reading time."

I kept my eye on Amir the rest of the time, watching him sit up straight, smile, and jot something down on his organizer as he read. When I went back at the end of the reading time, he had figured out that it was time for Geronimo's vacation—but everyone at the newspaper where he worked depended on him. As he was showering to leave for trip #1, the phone rang, he had to rush back to his office, and he missed his plane. "So, what is Geronimo's problem?" I asked.

"His work keeps calling him for help, and then he misses his plane," Amir explained. Finally, he understood.

For that day, Amir had made progress. But he will still need regular conferences, and his responses will need to be daily. As soon as he seems confused again, a conference will be used to add one more piece of the reading puzzle so that he can begin to understand all on his own. That is how to fatten a starving reader—one reading snack at a time.

Getting Delayed Readers on Their Way

Delayed readers need to strengthen their reading muscles. People who have tried to tone their out-of-shape bodies know that this is often more work than pleasure, until the results of the efforts can be seen and they can feel good about the time they have devoted to improving their health and appearance. Every time delayed readers meet with success and realize that they themselves are capable of meeting a reading challenge and overcoming it, they move closer to true reading independence. Teachers should focus on making themselves dispensable to these growing readers. By supporting both these readers' skills *and* their self-confidence, they are being set on the path to a lifetime of joyful reading.

Common Teaching Points in Conferences with Delayed Readers

General Reading Hints

- When readers come to words they don't know, they read ahead to see if they need these words before spending too much time trying to decode them.
- Readers preview books before they begin reading so they know what to expect from the text.
- Everything in a text is there on purpose. Readers should think about why the author included what has just been read.
- Readers combine the information on the page with things they know from their own experience to "read between the lines" and see what the author is trying to tell us.
- Readers finish most books they read.
- Readers sometimes abandon books they don't like, but they can name specific things that made the book a bad choice for them.

Fiction Texts

- Fiction texts follow a predictable structure, the "plot mountain." Readers can use knowledge of this structure to help them know what to expect next from the text.
- Readers are often a bit confused at the beginning of fiction texts. Reading farther trying to determine the characters, the setting, and the problem will help clear up these confusions.
- Readers learn about the characters in a book by paying attention to the author's descriptions, to the character's words and actions, to what other people say about the character, and to how others react to that person.

- Every story must have a problem. The problem is whatever stands between the main character and that person's goal. The problem can be another person, something in nature, something in the society, or something in the characters themselves.
- Readers constantly use the ideas the author has presented to make predictions about what will happen next, but they are willing to change their predictions if the author provides new information.
- Historical fiction is set in the past. The reader should expect to see vocabulary that names things that existed in the past that may not be in existence today.
- Science fiction is set in the future. The reader will have to use imagination and the author's descriptions to picture things that don't currently exist.
- Readers use the author's words to picture what is happening in a story.
- Readers wonder about characters and events in a story. Making "I wonder" statements pushes the reading forward.
- Readers think about how the characters, setting, and events in a story are like things in their own lives. Making these connections moves the reading forward.
- Readers change their ideas about characters and events when the author provides new information.

Nonfiction Texts

- Nonfiction texts are written to provide information. Readers preview nonfiction to know what to expect from the text.
- The graphics in nonfiction texts are there to provide a great deal of information in a short space. Readers should read these graphics to gain more information.
- Nonfiction texts contain what is called specialized vocabulary, words that are used only when talking about the particular subject of the text. Readers expect to find these words and use context clues or a glossary to figure out their meaning.
- Nonfiction texts often contain glossaries to help with difficult, specialized vocabulary.
- Informational texts do not have to be read from cover to cover. Instead, readers can skip around in these texts and read what is interesting to them.

- Biographies must be read from cover to cover because they are in time order and read like a story.
- The purpose of a biography is to give readers information about a person's life. These texts do not follow the plot structure of fiction because their purpose is to give information, not tell a story.
- Readers can always tell what new information they learned from reading a nonfiction text.

References

Agnes, M. (Ed.). (2002). *Webster's New World College Dictionary, 4th ed.* Cleveland, OH: Wiley Publishing.

Brownlee, S. (1999, August 9). Inside the teen brain. *U.S. News & World Report,* 44–54.

Caine, R. N., & Caine, G. (1994). *Making connections: Teaching and the human brain.* Menlo Park, CA: Addison-Wesley.

Carlsen, G. R. (1994). "Literature IS . . ." In A. Sherrill & T. C. Ley (Eds.), *Literature IS . . .: Collected essays by G. Robert Carlsen* (pp. 7–12). Johnson City, TN: Sabre Printers.

Goldman, D. (1995). *Emotional intelligence.* New York: Bantam.

LeDoux, J. (1996). *The emotional brain: The mysterious underpinnings of emotional life.* New York: Touchstone.

Sylwester, R. (1995). *A celebration of neurons: An educator's guide to the human brain.* Alexandria, VA: Association for Supervision and Curriculum Development.

Trade Books Cited

Cleary, B. (1968). *Ramona the pest.* New York: Avon.

Dadey, D., & Jones, M. T. The *Bailey School Kids* series. New York: Scholastic.

Stilton, G. (2004). *Geronimo Stilton #9: A fabumouse vacation for Geronimo.* New York: Scholastic.

Weston, C. (2000). *The diary of Melanie Martin or how I survived Matt the brat, Michelangelo, and the leaning tower of pizza.* New York: Dell Yearling.

Chapter 7

Conferencing with On-Level Readers

*Y*ou have to remember to look and to pay attention. Buried somewhere under all those government regulations that direct your attention to your neediest students, hidden there behind passing test scores and disguised by passing grades are your on-level students. They are easy to overlook in this current day and time—but they, too, deserve support and attention. They, too, need to grow as readers.

The Elementary and Secondary Education Act of 2001, better known as No Child Left Behind, is a well-intentioned piece of legislation. Its expressed purpose is "to close the achievement gap with accountability, flexibility, and choice, so that no child is left behind" (Section 1: Short Title, ¶ 1).

For too long, educators accepted the fact that some students just weren't achieving and offered many logical reasons why this was true. It is no wonder that politicians have called educators to task and forced them to raise their expectations. However, all the current emphasis on students who are not reaching expected levels of proficiency leaves those who are at grade level in the shadows. If all the attention is directed to those who are behind, what will happen to those who have—to this point—kept up? Tomlinson (1999) reminds us: "*Every* child [emphasis mine] is entitled to the promise of a teacher's enthusiasm, time, and energy" (p. 21).

Because teachers must focus more and more attention on below-level readers in order to meet the demands of current legislation, many on-level readers have been left mostly to their own devices. They are often taken for granted—

just give them a book and ask them to read it and all will be well. All is *not* well with many of these readers; they are often some of the most disengaged readers in the room. No one has shown interest in their reading in a while because they are doing just fine—so they often take very little interest in reading themselves. Although these students are very capable of reading, they often choose not to. Lesesne (2006) maintains that 75% of graduating seniors in high school vow to never read a book again. Surely, teachers want a better reading future than this for the students with whom they work. Engagement must be a focus of deskside conferences, particularly for on-level readers.

There is a real danger that on-level students will stall in their development if they, too, are not provided with focused instruction designed to help them grow. Fountas and Pinnell (2001) point out that texts at advanced levels include more complex sentences, more multisyllabic words, more sophisticated and mature themes and ideas, and more literary features, such as figurative and literary language. Readers are asked to do increasingly more inferring and to track ever more numerous characters and subplots. Theme, symbolism, tone, and mood assume more and more importance. If teachers decide that these readers no longer need their help, these students are in danger of being like the baseball player who is so excited about the ball he hit over the leftfield fence for a walk-off homerun that he forgets to tag home plate as he goes by. Teachers have celebrated too early—and their students are the ones who will pay.

The Needs of On-Level Readers

By the time they reach the intermediate grades, on-level readers have mastered the skill of decoding. They will, like all readers, sometimes encounter words that are unfamiliar and may have trouble pronouncing them, but they will at least be able to make a credible attempt. They will understand how fiction texts are constructed, though they may still find non-narrative expository texts challenging. Many of them, however, are stuck in a genre or in a series; many are only going through the motions. Their ability to perform at expected levels has given them the enviable ability to fly under the radar—and unless teachers realize that their needs are worthy of focused attention, these readers are in danger of stalling out and failing to make continued progress.

Students who are proficient in grade-level texts may continue to read at this comfortable level and not make the leap to more sophisticated reading unless supported by a more skilled reader who can help them manage the challenges higher level texts provide. Because supported independent reading gives teachers time to work with every reader in the room, they are better able to meet the needs of these proficient, but still growing, readers.

A Conference with a Book Trader

Book traders are readers who have never learned that reading can be fun. They will read when asked to—but *only* when asked to. Often, they are at or near grade level and can even function relatively well in the painfully difficult world of textbook reading—but they will never *choose* to read. It holds no attraction for them whatsoever.

It is not hard to recognize these readers. They are the ones who will s-l-o-w-l-y log in on their reading logs or dig in their desks for a few minutes at the start of reading time, just to shorten the amount of time they actually have to spend reading. Often, they will sigh as they open their books. They will glance at the clock at regular intervals, as if willing the 30 minutes of reading time to mercifully be over. They won't be discipline problems and will complete the reading log and response—but they will basically just be going through the motions. It isn't that they *can't* read—they just don't want to.

In a classroom that sets students completely free during independent reading time, these students will get lost in the shuffle. They will continue to dutifully perform when asked—but they will never become the readers they could be unless someone helps them learn that reading can take them on glorious adventures and help them better understand their world.

Book traders change books—a lot! Monday, they may be reading a graphic novel; on Tuesday, they may have a fantasy book; on Wednesday, they may be sitting with a nonfiction text—and on it goes. They will have a constant parade of books to fill their reading logs—and may even finish one or two from time to time. But basically, they are just filling their minds with words each day—and none of those words is considered particularly interesting.

Teachers need to be determined that no students ever leave their classrooms without finding a book they love. *No* students—period! Every person in the world can be transformed into a true reader by finding exactly the right book at precisely the right moment or, as Lesesne (2003) terms it, "making the match." My focus for conferences with book traders is always on engagement, on finding exactly that precisely right book.

A conference with a book trader always begins with either "What are you reading today?" or "Do you like your book so far?" These questions form a good bridge for the teaching that will be done after the student answers.

Jonathan is a book trader. He often has huge stacks of books piled on his desk for independent reading—and may even "read" each one during the 30 minutes unless I can get to him in time. One day recently he proudly showed me the five—no kidding—Lemony Snicket books he had stacked on his desk while he thumbed through a graphic novel he had borrowed from someone else. To Jonathan, just having the books and skimming through them is enough.

Jonathan is a fairly capable reader. He can—when he chooses to—perform adequately on assignments. The problem is that that is not usually the choice he makes.

The day I saw Jonathan borrowing a book from someone else when he had all those books proudly stacked on his desk already is the day I declared war on his apathy. I just could not stand to watch him waste another 30 minutes of his day. I had seen him have urgent needs to suddenly sharpen his pencil, to dig in his tote tray, to polish his glasses, to get a tissue for his nose. I had corrected his off-task behavior *ad nauseum*—and I was done. I was now on a mission to redefine Jonathan's relationship with texts.

I walked up to Jonathan's desk, clipboard in hand, and said, "Wow! That's a lot of books you have there! Which one are you reading?"

He proudly held up a *Dragon Knights* book and replied, "This one. I borrowed it from Adam."

"I'm surprised you needed to borrow one since you already had so many on your desk," I commented.

"Well, I've already read all of these."

"You have?" I said enthusiastically. "Which one did you like the best?"

Jonathan began to shuffle through his stack of *Unfortunate Adventures*, telling me the titles of each and which number they were in the series. It was not too hard to provide that information, since the books were sitting right there on the desk!

"But which one did you enjoy the most?" I asked again.

Again, the litany of titles and numbers. Finally, I stopped him. "Jonathan," I said. "I'm asking you to tell me what *happened* in the one you liked the best."

Silence.

Jonathan's whole personality changed in an instant. Where he had been animated before, he was now totally lethargic. He looked down at his desk, his shoulders sagged, and he began to shift in his chair. He had been caught in a lie—and he knew it.

My initial thought was that I wanted to nail Jonathan for the lie—but being his accuser would not help me in my quest to be his guide. The next thing I said could not be critical—and I knew it.

"Jonathan," I said quietly. "I am so glad that you're interested in so many books. I don't expect you to have read so many so fast. If you had done that, you couldn't possibly have taken the time to enjoy every one. Let's see if I can help you get started on one of these."

My words were carefully chosen. I wanted to build on what Jonathan had done well—find books in which he was interested—and guide him to the next logical step—actually reading one. In the meantime, I had to point out where his thinking was skewed—that just collecting books and pretending to read them was not enough. I had to do this in a nonthreatening way if I was going to positively impact his view of reading.

I spent the next 5 minutes or so letting Jonathan choose a book to read, previewing it, and reminding him that at the beginning of books, authors are going to give us important information about the characters, setting, and problem—and we have to be looking for those clues. We read the first two or three pages together, shared questions we had about what would happen next, and then I turned Jonathan loose to read on his own.

Did this conference magically change his life? Of course not. It took several years for Jonathan to become this disengaged, and I am realistic enough to know I'm not going to turn it around in a 10-minute conference. Jonathan continues to want to change books, and I continue to monitor his reading and redirect his thinking. He still is not finishing enough books to satisfy me, but he is finishing *some*—and that is progress. I continue to notice the types of books he's choosing and to talk to him about why he has made those choices. I get a clearer picture of his interests every day. And every day, I remind him that his job is to choose books he will finish and enjoy.

When faced with challenges such as Jonathan, teachers must keep their own attitudes positive by remembering that these are children. Even if they are six-foot-two, they are still children learning to read. Children exhibit behaviors that are not acceptable in the adult world, and it is the job of the adults around them to help them learn more appropriate behaviors. They don't learn through confrontation; they learn through redirection.

Teachers must then take the time to get the students involved in the beginning of a book by reading with them and modeling how readers use questions to drive their reading forward. It may take several days of modeling this type of reading at the point in the text where the student has stalled to get students truly invested in the books they have chosen. By paying attention to the types of books these readers are choosing, teachers can be armed with books that might engage these readers if they lose interest in what they themselves have brought. Always, the focus must be on engagement—these students need to learn to be hooked on reading.

A Conference with a Page Turner

Page turners are students who are perfectly willing to have a book, log it in on their reading logs, hold it in front of them for 30 minutes, and regularly turn the pages. They just aren't willing to actually read it. They have been playing the independent reading game a long time—but the rules must change. The focus in these conferences should always be on the fact that reading is finding the author's meaning, not just looking at the words the author has put on the page.

Marcus is a page turner. He is a delightful young man—perpetually upbeat, socially strong with both adults and peers, compliant, and attentive. He just doesn't particularly like to read. His mother takes him to the city library and buys him books at book stores. He is *never* without a book—or a perceived intention to read it. The actual reading, however, often does not happen.

Marcus does not change books every day—he keeps one about the amount of time he figures I would believe it takes him to read it and then he produces a new one. His responses are skeletal, but sometimes close enough that they might not draw my attention. But when I ask him what's happened in his book so far, the lack of specificity in his responses clearly shows he is either not reading or not comprehending.

This particular day, Marcus was "reading" the biography of a wrestler. He had been "reading" it for a couple of days and was now on page 37. I approached his desk and said, "A wrestling book, huh? What have you learned that's interesting?"

"Well, there's this guy named Stone Cold Steve Austin, and he's a professional wrestler."

Obviously, Marcus knew this before he ever picked up the book, so I pushed harder. "What can you tell me about him?"

"Well, he's a really good wrestler. A lot of people really like him."

"Is that why you chose this book?"

"Yeah, I'm interested in pro wrestling."

"This book is a biography. Biographies help us learn what well-known people are like in their real lives. What have you learned about Steve Austin as a person?"

"He's a really good wrestler."

And so the cycle goes.

It could be that Marcus was just in a book he couldn't understand, but when I asked him to go back to the beginning and read the first several pages to me, it was clear that this book was a good choice for him—he just obviously hadn't

Conferencing with On-Level Readers

been reading it. His eyes may have been going across the words—but his mind had been elsewhere the whole time.

"Marcus," I began, "I feel like you haven't really been *reading* this book—you've just been holding the book and looking at the words. *Reading* in nonfiction means you've been trying to learn something from the words on the page—do you feel like you've learned very much?"

"Not really, Mrs. Allison," he admitted sheepishly.

"The good news is that that isn't happening because you *can't* read this book—you just haven't been doing it. Is that a fair thing to say?"

"Yes, ma'am."

"Okay—tell me what you want to do. Do you think you can start over with this book with the intention of actually reading it, or do you need to pick another?"

"I'll start this one over."

"Okay, that sounds like a good plan. I'm going to come back to you near the end of reading time and let you tell me what you've learned about Steve Austin today—okay? When we read nonfiction, we should *always* expect to learn something new."

Marcus now had a purpose for reading. There had been a clear explanation of what he should expect from biographies, and he was allowed to decide whether or not he would continue in the book he had. He will still need to be checked on regularly—when book holders know their teachers are serious about them actually reading, they usually actually read.

Remembering Our On-Level Readers

Because they are reading "on level," these readers are ready to branch out and explore new genres, learning what to expect from each one along the way. They have met educational expectations because they have been reading, but many have now reached a plateau and are rapidly losing interest in the books they once loved. They need the benefit of teachers who understand that readers go through predictable phases on their way to a lifelong dedication to reading. Students who once enjoyed chapter books in the phase known as "unconscious delight" (Carlsen, 1994) are now ready to move on to the phase where they read about people whose situations and problems are much like their own in a phase Lesesne (2006) has termed "reading autobiographically." Later, they will want to read about places and experiences they have never known and live out the adventures through characters in books, or they will want to explore philosophical issues that interest them (Carlsen, 1994). By understanding the progression of

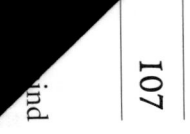

...lge these capable readers into new genres that may ...m on-track in their development.
...aders whose scores tell us they are proficient, we ...r proficiency may be minimal and in danger of ... help them engage with texts and learn more and ... ...s of reading they can explore. Our goal should be to help them read with a sense of joy rather than with a sense of duty, so that they will continue to be both capable and dedicated readers.

Common Teaching Points in Conferences with On-Level Readers

General Reading Hints

- Readers choose books that they plan to finish and enjoy.
- Readers read from a variety of genres, both fiction and nonfiction, written by a variety of authors.
- Readers choose continually more sophisticated books so that they will stay interested and grow as readers.
- Readers don't just say the words; they spend time thinking about what information the words are trying to give to the reader.
- Readers often get ideas for what to read next from the other readers around them.

Fiction Texts

- Many fiction texts have multiple plot lines that the reader must track. Readers always expect these plots to come together near the end of the book.
- Readers think about why the author made the characters the way they are. They think ahead to how a character's personality might affect the events in the story.
- Authors choose their settings for a reason. Readers think about why the story is set in a certain time and place and how this setting will affect the events to come.

- In very complicated stories with many settings and characters, readers sometimes keep lists of characters or places to help keep these details straight.
- In complicated texts, authors sometimes give maps or character trees at the beginning of the book so readers can refer back to these if they get confused.
- Large spaces between blocks of text usually indicate a change in setting or event.
- Authors sometimes use italics to show when a character is thinking rather than speaking.
- Authors sometimes play with time, including what are called flashbacks, to give the reader more understanding of a character or situation.

Nonfiction Texts

- Readers sometimes take the time to look something up in a reference book if understanding a term, place, or person is important to understanding a text.
- Narrative nonfiction texts read like a story, but they do not follow the plot structure of fiction because their purpose is to give information rather than to just tell a story.
- The index in a nonfiction book can help readers find the information in which they are interested.
- Readers go into informational texts with an idea about what they want to learn. Often, these ideas are phrased as questions that drive the reading forward.
- Readers stop often while reading nonfiction to think about what new things they have learned.
- The more background knowledge readers have about the subject of nonfiction, the easier the text will be to read.

References

http://www.ed.gov/policy/elsec/leg/esea02/beginning.html#sec1. Retrieved May 12, 2006.

Carlsen, G. R. (1994). "Literature IS . . ." In A. Sherrill & T. C. Ley (Eds.), *Literature IS . . .: Collected essays by G. Robert Carlsen* (pp. 7–12). Johnson City, TN: Sabre Printers.

Fountas, I. C., & Pinnell, G. S. (2001). *Guiding readers & writers, grades 3–6.* Portsmouth, NH: Heinemann.

Lesesne, T. S. (2003). *Making the match.* Portland, ME: Stenhouse.

Lesesne, T. S. (2006). *Naked reading: Uncovering what tweens need to become lifelong readers.* Portland, ME: Stenhouse.

Tomlinson, C. (1999). *The differentiated classroom: Responding to the needs of all learners.* Alexandria, VA: Association for Supervision and Curriculum Development.

United States Department of Education. (2001). Elementary and secondary education act. Retrieved June 15, 2006, from http://www.ed.gov/policy/elsec/leg/esea02/beginning.html#sec1.

Trade Books Cited

Burgan, M. (2001). *Stone cold: Pro wrestler Steve Austin.* Mankato, MN: Capstone.

Ohkami, M., Ichimura, Y., & DeMarle, M. (2002). *Dragon knights.* Los Angeles: TokyoPop.

Snicket, L. The *A Series of Unfortunate Events* series. New York: HarperCollins.

Chapter 8

Conferencing with Gifted Readers

A friend of mine who lives in a rural area near a city in the Midwest has a son who is profoundly gifted. When Ben was in elementary school, she called me one evening, totally frustrated. The neighborhood school had no program for students as far ahead of their peers as Ben, and their only method of meeting his needs was to bus him 30 minutes away to an elementary school in close proximity to a middle school where he could take some classes with students who were nowhere near his own age. His mother wanted to know if she had any legal recourse, and I'm afraid she didn't. Even though gifted students have just as many special needs as their learning-disabled classmates, the current emphasis on every child performing at grade level actually works against them. These students left grade level in the dust long ago. They are often given more work, rather than being given work at a higher intellectual level—and they are constantly be asked to help their struggling classmates, who often resent the help.

This is one reason why, according to DeLisle and Galbraith (2002), "Some of the most talented students in the United States actually choose to drop out of school altogether" (p. 28). Reis and McCoach (2002) list "underchallenging, slow-moving classroom experiences" (p. 83) and the need to conform to their peers as reasons why many gifted students suddenly become underachievers. In classrooms filled with students of varying abilities and interests, it is often the gifted child who becomes invisible to the teacher. These students can perform on grade level with very little effort, and much of their teachers' time and energy is focused on the students who are *not* performing as well.

Unless teachers make a commitment as educators to notice the gifted children with whom they are privileged to work and to offer them the same level of challenge placed in front of the other students in the room, they are, in fact, placing these students in environments that accept, and even encourage, their underachievement. Rimm (in Winebrenner, 2001) cautions that ". . . when gifted children lack motivation, it is not genetic but taught" (p. xi). Teachers have a professional responsibility to be sure that all the children with whom they work, including the gifted ones, are challenged in ways that lead them to see that hard work is necessary to develop their full potential. Even gifted children should be presented with challenges for which they will need teacher support and guidance. They should not be sent off to a corner of the classroom to work independently on assignments that fail to challenge them.

Finding books at appropriate reading levels for gifted intermediate students presents its own set of challenges, since many of the books at the proper level deal with issues and ideas that are far above the emotional maturity of these students. These higher level books are written for adolescents who are beginning to grapple with such things as identity and sexual encounters. Books written for this age are more graphic and contain more profanity than those written for younger students. There are, however, many books written at a lower reading level, such as Spinelli's (1990) *Maniac Magee*, that offer a great deal of complexity if the reader is prompted to look for it. These students are not too young to learn about things such as symbolism and motifs, as well as antiheroes.

Because supported independent reading individualizes instruction, it is a powerful vehicle for working with gifted students in a regular classroom setting. Supported independent reading gives these students a chance not only to move at their own pace, but also to dig more deeply into texts than their same-age peers. Many of the gifted students with whom I have worked trade speed reading for deep understanding. They can breeze through texts at a lightening pace, astounding their classmates with their ability to read the newest *Harry Potter* book in a weekend. But these students are not as challenged by reading longer texts as they could be by reading texts more deeply.

A Conference with a Speeding Reader

Felix is a speeding reader. If reading were a highway, he'd have been given so many tickets by now that he'd never drive again. Reading for him is effortless; he has been known to start, finish, *and* comprehend up to 10 books a week. He delights in taking books other students have finished and breezing through them in less than a day, *not* to the delight of his classmates. His entire reading identity seems to be tied up in reading faster and more prolifically than anyone else—but he is not seeing all the wonderful layers of meaning evident in many of the texts he is jetting through, even though he is intellectually capable of doing so.

One book he started during independent reading time and finished overnight was Louis Sachar's (1998) amazing *Holes*. This book has many layers of meaning and incredible artistic devices, including frequent flashbacks that wind up tying various storylines together. Felix had watched several classmates take 2 weeks or longer to read this book, but they had rejoiced in such things as discovering that Zero and Madame Z were related. Felix just read right through that part as if it weren't amazing at all.

The other students were astounded that he had finished that book overnight but felt somewhat vindicated when, uncharacteristically, he failed a test on it. Even that didn't seem to phase Felix. When I asked him why he thought he did so poorly on the test, he just said, "Maybe I read it too fast."

I wanted him to understand exactly how much he had missed. "Felix," I said, "*Holes* is one of the best books I've ever read. It is beautifully written and carefully structured, and every single detail is important. Sachar did a masterful job of creating characters we would love and dropping hints about how their pasts and their futures would intertwine. Did you catch *any* of that?"

"I like the book, Mrs. Allison," Felix said, eager to pick up the *Charlie Bones* book he had started today. "I just read it too fast. No big deal."

"Felix," I said, "it *is* a big deal. You are such a good reader—but you seem to think that reading a book quickly is more important than reading it well."

Felix looked at me like I had just landed from another planet. "I don't understand what you mean," he said.

"You read *Holes* in less than 24 hours. I'm a fast reader, too, but I slow down when I read beautifully written books so that I can think about all the incredible things the author has done. Even Stanley's name is a masterful touch—it's the same when read forward or backward. Every character's name is perfect and significant in some way. And the way he plays with time, using the past to drop hints about how Stanley's problem will eventually be solved—that book didn't just happen. It was carefully crafted by a master storyteller—and it deserved the Newbery award it won."

Felix continued to give me that creature-from-another-planet stare. "Great, Mrs. Allison, I'm glad you really liked that book. Now, can I get back to *Charlie Bones*?"

The first chapter of *Holes* is a masterpiece full of irony and intentionally short sentences. Felix could tell me that the story took place at Camp Green Lake but was reluctant to waste any energy on the reason why Sachar would have set this story in such an odd place. Even after I explained the idea of irony, Felix continued to be interested *only* in getting me to release him from any obligation of thought so he could fly through the *Charlie Bones* book sitting on his desk at the moment.

Felix already has enough problems relating to the mere mortals around him, none of whom understand his desire to be a paranormal investigator when he grows up, since none of them is quite sure what that is. Felix marches to a different drummer, as do many gifted students. His only connection to the students around him is his reading of the same books they read—he does not *want* to read them differently.

Speeding readers need to be slowed down *before* they begin a text. They need to be steered to texts that will lend themselves to a higher level of thought and an examination of author's craft (Fig. 8:1). Then, they must be given response assignments that help them master these higher level skills.

Holes by Louis Sachar
Walk Two Moons by Sharon Creech
The Last Book in the Universe by Rodman Philbrick
The Giver by Lois Lowry
The Westing Game by Ellen Raskin
Chasing Vermeer by Blue Balliett
Out of Nowhere by Ouida Sebestyen
Criss Cross by Lynne Rae Perkins
Whirlygig by Paul Fleischman
Things Not Seen by Andrew Clements
The Afterlife by Gary Soto
Kira, Kira by Cynthia Kadohata
Stargirl by Jerry Spinelli
Maniac Magee by Jerry Spinelli
The Outcasts of 19 Schulyer Place by E. L. Konigsburg
The Same Stuff as Stars by Katharine Paterson
Blackwater by Eve Bunting
Tangerine by Edward Bloor
The Only Alien on the Planet by Kristen D. Randle
The Tale of Despereaux by Kate DiCamillo
The Tiger Rising by Kate DiCamillo

Figure 8:1 Some books to focus gifted readers on higher level thinking.

Teachers must understand that these gifted readers may, at first, resist efforts to make them work harder and think more deeply. They are used to breezing through assignments that present little, if any, challenge. They are likely to be just as confused and misguided as some of the more challenged readers. If they must work to do what their teachers have asked, they are reading at a level that should help them grow. The goal is to create what Caine and Caine (1994) call "relaxed alertness," a level of challenge that is manageable enough to prevent frustration but advanced enough to create new learning. It is in this state that, according to Caine and Caine (1994), students are most likely to learn. Therefore, allowing gifted readers to continue to breeze through texts just to keep them occupied is not good educational practice.

Felix passed our state test with flying colors, to absolutely no one's surprise. But he is the student I feel I failed this school year. He deserved the same chance to read with me as a partner there to help guide him through challenges as the students did who were still struggling with *Ramona Quimby* and Junie B. Jones. He asked me one day why he was never included in any small reteaching groups, and I dutifully patted his back and told him because he didn't need to be retaught. No, he didn't need *re*teaching—he needed *different* teaching.

A Conference with a Lingering Reader

Serena, too, is a gifted reader—but as different from Felix as she can possibly be. Where Felix is the sprinter trying to get to the finish line first, Serena is the old lady out for a Sunday morning stroll, stopping all along the way to literally smell the roses. Serena is what I call a lingering reader, one who savors every moment spent in the world created by texts. She is in no hurry to reach the end—the joy is in the journey.

Readers such as Serena can become victims of a reading program that requires a certain number of books to be read in a certain amount of time. This requirement might spur reluctant readers to actually complete a book, but for readers such as Serena, it robs them of a chance to enjoy the journey.

Because Serena is a very advanced reader, she chooses very long books. She likes fantasy, as many gifted readers do, and had chosen Paolini's (2004) very popular *Eragon* as her book for independent reading. She soon became totally lost in the fantastic world the author had created, a world full of magic and dragons and adventure. The look on her face while she read was one of pure rapture—and I was reluctant to bother her. For several days, I just walked by her desk and smiled.

Finally, one day, Serena stopped me. "Wait, wait, Mrs. Allison," she began. "I want you to read this part." She pulled on my arm, and I knelt down beside her as she pointed to the section she wanted me to read. I knew nothing about this particular book, since fantasy is not a genre in which I choose to read often, so I asked her for a quick summary of what had happened so far.

Serena launched into a detailed and fascinating account of what had happened so far in the book. She was clearly enthralled by every character and every event in the novel. I had truly never seen a reader so thoroughly engaged with a text.

The next day, Serena was reading a different book, a mystery much shorter than *Eragon*. Puzzled, I stopped by her desk and asked why she had switched books.

"I have to have a book finished by Friday," she explained, "and I won't finish *Eragon* in time, so I'm going to read this one really fast so I can get back to it."

I, too, have required classes full of students to have a book finished by a certain date without ever considering how this might impact lingering readers, such as Serena. There are students who are far above their expected reading level who just want to carve out time during the day to lose themselves in a world very different from their own. Serena, too, has trouble relating to her classmates because her thinking is so far ahead of their own. But she does not need a teacher to prompt her to look at author's craft or to understand theme and symbolism—she has figured that out on her own already. All she needs is time—and artificial deadlines rob her of exactly what she needs.

Serena was released from the requirements of the deadline and allowed to read *Eragon* at her own pace. Because her engagement with and understanding of the text were never an issue, she was allowed to spend as much time with Paolini's words as she needed. She could have read it faster; she was choosing not to. She was choosing to savor every word and every event in this magical book. That is a choice she should have the freedom to make.

Besides needing to be given the gift of time, Serena also wanted someone to talk to about the book every now and then. The students around her were not at a place in their own reading where they could begin to understand her level of involvement with text, so it was important that I serve as her sounding board. I didn't have to remember to check in with her—she would literally grab me as I walked by when she had something new she wanted to share. And always, she began by enthusiastically catching me up on everything that had happened in the book since we had last talked. She just needed someone to listen; all readers deserve that.

Serena finished *Eragon* and got a 100 on the test. She then moved on to its sequel, *Eldest*, which her parents gave her for Christmas. It took Serena over 2 months to read the first book, but it was time well spent. She got more out of that one book during that time than any other reader got from the multiple texts finished during the same amount of time. And no reader in the room was more engaged than she was.

Lingering readers need to be given the freedom to read at their own pace and to savor the words on the page. They are not reading slowly because they are struggling to comprehend; they are reading slowly because they are enjoying the world the book has created for them. Once teachers have determined that this is the case, these readers need to be released from artificial deadlines. Deskside conferences with them should occur when these readers want to share—and even if their summaries are long and full of minutiae, teachers need to give them the time to tell their stories. This behavior honors true engagement.

Common Teaching Points in Conferences with Gifted Readers

General Reading Hints

- Reading faster does not always mean reading well.
- Readers sometimes like to slow down and enjoy particularly good writing.
- Readers should read from a variety of texts, both fiction and nonfiction, written by a variety of authors.
- Readers understand that the act of reading is a sort of game between authors and readers. Much is written between the lines, and readers must take the time to understand what is implied.

Fiction Texts

- Authors often put a character or object into a story as a symbol of a bigger idea. Readers always think about what these things might represent.
- Sometimes, seemingly simple stories actually represent bigger issues. Readers often think about what point authors are really trying to make.
- Good fiction has a theme, or point, it is trying to make. Readers are always thinking about what this point might be.

- Authors do everything in fiction on purpose. Readers constantly think about why characters have certain traits or why certain events were included.
- Readers always make connections between what they are currently reading and books they have read before that are similar. They look for similarities in characters, in problems, and in resolutions.
- Readers pay attention to what the author does to make the text of good quality. Paying attention to the author's craft makes them both better readers and better writers.
- Readers sometimes read several books by the same author, looking for what similarities there are between the books.

Nonfiction Texts

- Readers choose to read about a topic because they want deep, rather than surface, knowledge about something.
- Readers enjoy knowing specific details about things that interest them.
- Readers sometimes read several books on the same subject and compare the various authors' ideas and presentation styles.
- Readers think about how authors decide what information to put into a book and what information to leave out.
- Readers consider how an author's point of view about a subject determines how the information is presented.
- Readers look for authors' bias as they read informational texts.

References

Caine, R. N., & Caine, G. (1994). *Making connections: Teaching and the human brain.* Menlo Park, CA: Addison-Wesley.

DeLisle, J., & Galbraith, J. (2002). *When gifted kids don't have all the answers.* Minneapolis, MN: Free Spirit.

Reis, S. M., & McCoach, D. B. (2002). Underachievement in gifted students. In M. Neihart, S. M. Reis, N. M. Robinson, & S. M. Moon (Eds.), *The social and emotional development of gifted children* (pp. 81–91). Washington, DC: National Association for Gifted Children.

Winebrenner, S. (2001). *Teaching gifted kids in the regular classroom.* Minneapolis, MN: Free Spirit.

Trade Books Cited

Balliett, B. (2005). *Chasing Vermeer*. New York: Scholastic.
Bloor, E. (1997). *Tangerine*. New York: Scholastic.
Bunting, E. (1999). *Blackwater*. New York: HarperTrophy.
Clements, A. (2002). *Things not seen*. New York: Puffin.
Creech, S. (1994). *Walk two moons*. New York: HarperCollins.
DiCamillo, K. (2003). *The tale of despereaux*. Cambridge, MS: Candlewick.
DiCamillo, K. (2002). *The tiger rising*. Cambridge, MS: Candlewick.
Fleischman, P. (1998). *Whirlygig*. New York: Dell Laurel-Leaf.
Kadohata, C. (2004). *Kira, kira*. New York: Atheneum.
Konigsburg, E. L. (2004). *The outcasts of 19 Schulyer Place*. New York: Atheneum.
Lowry, L. (1993). *The giver*. New York: Houghton Mifflin.
Nimmo, J. The *Charlie Bones* series. New York: Orchard.
Paolini, C. (2004). *Eragon*. New York: Knopf Books for Young Readers.
Paterson, K. (2002). *The same stuff as stars*. New York: Clarion.
Perkins, L. R. (2005). *Criss cross*. New York: HarperCollins.
Philbrick. R. (2000). *The last book in the universe*. New York: Scholastic.
Randle, K. D. (1996). *The only alien on the planet*. New York: Scholastic.
Raskin, E. (1978). *The westing game*. New York: Penguin.
Sachar, L. (1998). *Holes*. New York: Dell Yearling.
Sebestyen, O. (1994). *Out of nowhere*. New York: Puffin.
Soto, G. (2003). *The afterlife*. New York: Harcourt.
Spinelli, J. (1990). *Maniac magee*. New York: Little Brown.
Spinelli, J. (2000). *Stargirl*. New York: Alford A. Knopf.

Appendix A

Fascinating You

Help me get to know you better by writing about what makes you *you*. There is only one you in the world—and that is what makes *you* so interesting!

This will be draft writing, so don't worry too much right now about your spelling and punctuation. These things will be important later, when we write some things to share with a wider audience. But this writing is just for me—and I can usually figure out what you're trying to say. And it is what you're saying that interests me—so put some thought into what you're writing, please!

No one will read this but me—so please be honest. The better I know you, the better I can teach you!

Paragraph 1: Tell me about your family.

- With whom do you live?
- How old are your brothers and sisters? Do you get along—or does your little brother or older sister drive you crazy? Explain, please!!
- Have you ever lived anywhere else? If so, where—and for how long? Did you like living there? Why or why not?
- Do you have any pets? Tell me their names and what they are like.

Paragraph 2: Tell me how you spend your free time.

- Do you play sports? If so, which ones—and what position(s) do you play? Which sport is your favorite?
- Do you play any musical instruments—and do you enjoy that? Why or why not?
- What are your favorite television programs—and why?
- Who are your favorite singers? What do you like about their music?

- Are you involved in any other activities—church groups, volunteer work, scouts? What kinds of things do you do with these groups, and what makes you enjoy them?
- Do you have family activities that you enjoy—camping, board games, visiting museums, family vacations? What types of things do you do together—and which are your favorites?

Paragraph 3: Tell me about your friends.
- Where did you meet your best friends? How long ago?
- What kinds of things do you and your friends like to do together?

Paragraph 4: Tell me about your summer.
- Did you take any trips? If so, where—and what did you enjoy most about the trip?
- What was your typical day like this summer? What did you do on an average day?
- How did you feel when you knew it was time to come back to school? Were you excited? Depressed? Nervous? Why did you feel this way?

Paragraph 5: Tell me what you expect from me.
- What kinds of assignments help you learn?
- What did the best teachers you've ever had do that you'd like me to do as well?
- What do you want to be sure I *don't* do because it will keep us from being able to work together well?

Appendix B

Daily Reading Log

Week of _____

Date	Title/Author	Page Started	Page Finished

Total number of pages read: _____
Total number of books finished: _____

Appendix C

Sample Notes from Conferencing

Aaron

10/1—Reading *Animorphs—The Visitor*—page 13
10/2—Same book. Page 15. Asked what was happening—seemed confused. Wasn't visualizing so didn't realize what had happened. Read aloud—he pictured and understood. Sticky to mark visualizations.
10/3—Had two stickies for images. Seems to be helping. Page 27
10/4—page 38
10/5—page 50

Trisha

10/1—Reading *Poppleton Has Fun*—has already finished *Poppleton*.
10/2—100 on AR test. Reading another Poppleton book. Bring *Gooseberry Park*.
10/3—100 again. Loaned *GP*.
10/4—*GP*—Page 25.

Anh

10/1—Reading *Face on the Milk Carton* as part of book group—on chapter 6
10/3—Chapter 8
10/5—Chapter 11

Jose

10/1—Reading Stone Cold—wrestling bio. Can only tell me what already knew. Is ignoring graphics. Asked to start over—list interesting new facts learned.
10/2—Recorded no facts yesterday. Started again. Took turns stopping when learned something new. Same assignment.
10/3—Still no new facts. Read one paragraph at time—stopped to retell. Is to have five facts by Friday.
10/4—Has two facts. Reminded of assignment.
10/5—Five facts. Took AR test—50%.

Michael

10/1—Reading *Face on the Milk Carton* as part of book group—on chapter 5
10/3—Chapter 6—Talked about being behind. Says likes book. Said would read extra time tonight to catch up.
10/4—Chapter 9—yea!

LaToya

10/2—Reading Abby Hayes—has read one before. Can name things she expects to see in the book. Page 27
10/3—page 33
10/4—page. 48—named favorite part.
10/5—page. 70

Kendrick

10/2—Reading *Night of the Twisters*—seems disinterested.
10/3—Reading *Save Queen of Sheba*—can't retell. Didn't realize was historical fiction. Sent to classroom library for new book. Picked Joey Pigza.
10/4—Reading Stone Cold bio. Talked about abandoning books. Must finish book he is reading at end of period. Gave four choices. Talked about confusions at beginning of books—what to expect.
10/5—Began *Fried Worms*. Read aloud—I stopped him to have him notice characters, setting, and situation. Page 8.

Lisa

10/2—Reading *Eragon*. Says she likes fantasy. Can tell me some characteristics of genre. Page 34.
10/5—*Eragon*—page 107.

Leroy

10/3—Reading *Goosebumps*. Has read four others in series. Page 51.
10/4—page 89
10/5—Took AR test. Got a 90. Recommended Wright or Hahn.

Malik

10/2—Reading *Face on the Milk Carton* as part of book group. On chapter 7. Bought *Whatever Happened to Janie*.
10/4—Chapter 11.

Appendix D

Book Pass Record Sheet

Author	Title	Genre	Too Easy	Just Right	Too Hard

—adapted from Janet Allen *Yellow Brick Roads*

Appendix D (continued)

Character Clue Collection (Intermediate Version)

Title of book:
Author:
Name of character:

What He/She Looks Like	What He/She Says	What He/She Does	What He/She Thinks	How Others React to Him/Her

Appendix E

Character Clue Collection (Middle School Version)

Title of book:
Author:
Name of character:

Direct Description	Conversation	Actions	Thoughts	Reactions to Him/Her

Appendix F

Books I Want to Read

Title	Author	Call Number for Nonfiction

Appendix G

Connecting to the Character

Title of book:
Author:
Character's name:

Examples from the Book	Trait We Share	Examples from My Life

Appendix H

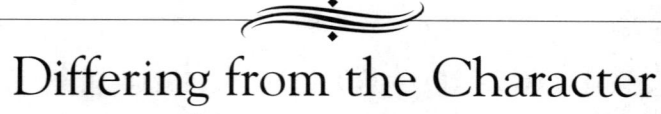

Differing from the Character

Title of book:
Author:
Character's name:

Character Trait and Example from Text	Opposite Trait and Example from My Life

Appendix I

The Author's Craft

Title of book:
Author:
Character's name:

Character Trait	Effect on the Story

Appendix J

Plot Structure "Plot Mountain"

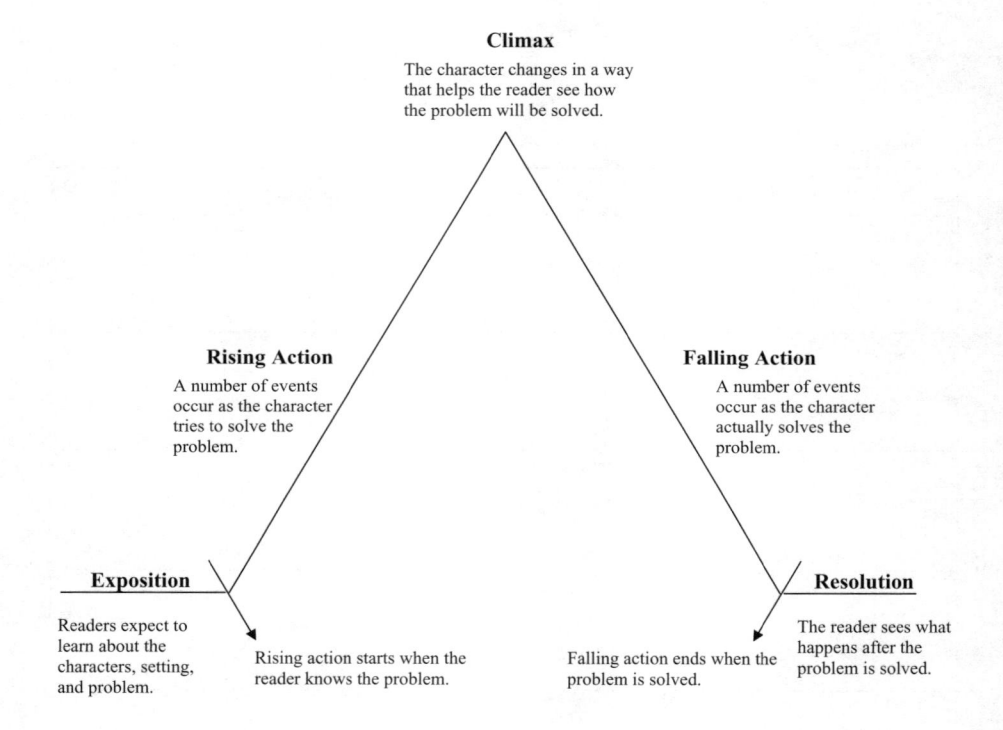

Climax
The character changes in a way that helps the reader see how the problem will be solved.

Rising Action
A number of events occur as the character tries to solve the problem.

Falling Action
A number of events occur as the character actually solves the problem.

Exposition
Readers expect to learn about the characters, setting, and problem.

Rising action starts when the reader knows the problem.

Falling action ends when the problem is solved.

Resolution
The reader sees what happens after the problem is solved.

References

Agnes, M. (Ed.). (2002). *Webster's New World College Dictionary, 4th ed.* Cleveland, OH: Wiley Publishing.

Allen, J. (2000). *Yellow brick roads. Shared and guided paths to independent reading 4–12.* Portland, ME: Stenhouse.

Allington, R. L. (2001). *What really matters for struggling readers: Designing research-based programs.* New York: Addison-Wesley.

Bear, D. R., Invernizzi, M., Templeton, S. R., & Johnston, F. (2003). *Words their way.* New York: Prentice Hall.

Beers, K. (1998). Choosing not to read: Understanding why some middle schoolers just say no. In K. Beers & B. G. Samuels (Eds.), *Into focus: Understanding and creating middle school readers* (pp. 37–63). Norwood, MA: Christopher-Gordon.

Brownlee, S. (1999, August 9). Inside the teen brain. *U.S. News & World Report,* 44–54.

Caine, R. N., & Caine, G. (1994). *Making connections: Teaching and the human brain.* Menlo Park, CA: Addison-Wesley.

Caine, R. N., & Caine, G. (1994). *Making connections: Teaching and the human brain.* Menlo Park, CA: Addison-Wesley.

Calkins, L. M. (2001). *The art of teaching reading.* New York: Addison-Wesley.

Carlsen, G. R. (1994). "Literature IS…" In A. Sherrill & T. C. Ley (Eds), *Literature IS . . .: Collected essays by G. Robert Carlsen* (pp. 7–12). Johnson City, TN: Sabre Printers.

Carter, B., & Abrahamson, R. F. (1998). Castles to Colin Powell: The truth about nonfiction. In K. Beers & B. G. Samuels (Eds.), *Into focus: Understanding and creating middle school readers* (pp. 313–331). Norwood, MA: Christopher-Gordon.

Carver, R. P. (2000). *The causes of high and low reading achievement.* Mahwah, NJ: Lawrence Erlbaum.

Daniels, H., & Bizar, M. (2005). *Teaching the best practice way: Methods that matter, K–12.* Portland, ME: Stenhouse.

DeLisle, J., & Galbraith, J. (2002). *When gifted kids don't have all the answers.* Minneapolis, MN: Free Spirit.

Fountas, I. C., & Pinnell, G. S. (2001). *Guiding readers and writers grades 3–6.* Portsmouth, NH: Heinemann.

Gallagher, M., & Pearson, P. D. (1983). The instruction of reading comprehension: *Contemporary Educational Psychology, 8,* 317–344.

Goldman, D. (1995). *Emotional intelligence.* New York: Bantam.

Guthrie, J. T., & Knowles, K. T. (2001). Promoting reading motivation. In L. Verhoeven & C. Snow (Eds.), *Literacy and motivation: Reading engagement in individuals and groups* (pp. 159–176). Mahwah, NJ: Lawrence Erlbaum.

Harvey, S., & Goudvis, A. (2000). *Strategies that work.* York, ME: Stenhouse.

http://www.ed.gov/policy/elsec/leg/esea02/beginning.html#sec1. Retrieved May 12, 2006.

Jensen, E. (1998). *Teaching with the brain in mind.* Alexandria, VA: Association for Supervision and Curriculum Development.

Jobe, R., & Dayton-Sakari, M. (1999). *Reluctant readers.* Markham, Ontario, Canada: Pembroke.

Keene, E. O., & Zimmerman, S. (1997). *Mosaic of thought: Teaching comprehension in a reader's workshop.* Portsmouth, NH: Heinemann.

Krashen, S. D. (2004). *The power of reading: Insights from research.* Portsmouth, NH: Heinemann.

LeDoux, J. (1996). *The emotional brain: The mysterious underpinnings of emotional life.* New York: Touchstone.

Lesesne, T. S. (2003). *Making the match.* Portland, ME: Stenhouse.

Lesesne, T. S. (2006). *Naked reading: Uncovering what tweens need to become lifelong readers.* Portland, ME: Stenhouse.

Lyons, C. A. (2003). *Teaching struggling readers.* Portsmouth, NH: Heinemann.

McKenna, M. C. (2001). Development of reading attitudes. In L. Verhoeven & C. Snow (Eds.), *Literacy and motivation: Reading engagement in individuals and groups* (pp. 135–158). Mahwah, NJ: Lawrence Erlbaum.

Probst, R. (1998). Reader–response theory in the middle school. In K. Beers & B. G. Samuels, (Eds.), *Into focus* (pp. 125–138). Norwood, MA: Christopher-Gordon.

Reis, S. M., & McCoach, D. B. (2002). Underachievement in gifted students. In M. Neihart, S. M. Reis, N. M. Robinson, & S. M. Moon (Eds.), *The social and emotional development of gifted children* (pp. 81–91). Washington, DC: National Association for Gifted Children.

Rosenblatt, L. (1995). *Literature as exploration.* New York: Modern Language Association.

Routman, R. (2003). *Reading essentials.* Portsmouth, NH: Heinemann.

Sibberson, F., & Szymusiak, K. (2003). *Still learning to read: Teaching students in grades 3–6.* Portland, ME: Stenhouse.

Sylwester, R. (1995). *A celebration of neurons: An educator's guide to the human brain.* Alexandria, VA: Association for Supervision and Curriculum Development.

Tomlinson, C. (1999). *The differentiated classroom: Responding to the needs of all learners.* Alexandria, VA: Association for Supervision and Curriculum Development.

United States Department of Education. (2001). Elementary and secondary education act. Retrieved June 15, 2006, from http://www.ed.gov/policy/elsec/leg/esea02/beginning.html#sec1.

Vygotsky, L. S. (1978). *Mind in society: The development of higher psychological processes.* Cambridge, MA: Harvard University Press.

Vygotsky, L. S. (1986). *Thought and language.* Cambridge, MA: MIT Press.

Winebrenner, S. (2001). *Teaching gifted kids in the regular classroom.* Minneapolis, MN: Free Spirit.

Worthy, J. (1996). Removing barriers to voluntary reading: The role of school and classroom libraries. *Language Arts, 73,* 484–492.

Trade Books Cited

Adler, D. A. (2002). *Cam Jansen and the birthday mystery.* East Rutherford, NJ: Puffin.

Applegate, K. The *Animorphs* series. New York: Scholastic.

Balliett, B. (2005). *Chasing Vermeer.* New York: Scholastic.

Bledsoe, G., & Bledsoe, K. (2002). *The world's fastest truck (built for speed).* Mankato, MN: Capstone.

Bloom, B. (1999). *Wolf!* New York: Scholastic.

Bloor, E. (1997). *Tangerine.* New York: Scholastic.

Bronte, E. (1983). *Wuthering Heights.* New York: Bantam Classics.

Bunting, E. (1999). *Blackwater.* New York: HarperTrophy.

Burgan, M. (2001). *Stone cold: Pro wrestler Steve Austin.* Mankato, MN: Capstone.
Cleary, B. The *Ramona Quimby* series. New York: HarperCollins.
Cleary, B. (1968). *Ramona the pest.* New York: Avon.
Clements, A. (2002). *Things not seen.* New York: Puffin.
Colfer, E. (2001). *Artemis fowl.* New York: Hyperion.
Conrad, P. (1991). *Stonewords.* New York: HarperCollins.
Cooney, C. B. (1991). *The face on the milk carton.* New York: Laurel Leaf.
Creech, S. (1996). *Walk two moons.* New York: HarperTrophy.
Dadey, D., & Jones, M. T. The *Bailey School Kids* series. New York: Scholastic.
Dahl, R. (1998). *The twits.* London: Puffin.
Danziger, P. The *Amber Brown* series. New York: Scholastic.
DiCamillo, K. (2003). *The tale of despereaux.* New York: Scholastic.
DiCamillo, K. (2002). *The tiger rising.* Cambridge, MA: Candlewick.
Fleischman, P. (1998). *Whirlygig.* New York: Dell Laurel-Leaf.
Franzen, J. (2002). *The corrections.* New York: Picador.
Gantos, J. (2000). *Joey Pigza swallowed the key.* New York: HarperTrophy.
Hahn, M. D. (1995). *Ghosts beneath our feet.* New York: Scholastic.
Hughes, M. The *Creepy creatures* series. Orlando, FL: Raintree.
Jacques, B. (1988). *Mossflower.* New York: Philomel Books.
Jacques, B. (1998). *Redwall.* New York: Ace.
Jones, E. P. (2004). *The known world.* New York: Amistad.
Kadohata, C. (2004). *Kira, kira.* New York: Atheneum.
Konigsburg, E. L. (2004). *The outcasts of 19 Schulyer Place.* New York: Atheneum.
Lee, H. (1988). *To kill a mockingbird.* New York: Warner Books.
Levine, G. C. (1997). *Ella enchanted.* New York: HarperCollins.
Lowry, L. (1993). *The giver.* New York: Houghton Mifflin.
Lyon, G. E. (1998). *A sign.* New York: Orchard.
Lyon, G. E. (1999). *Book.* New York: DK Children.
Mann, J. (2004). *The rise of the vulcans.* New York: Viking.
Masoff, J. (2000). *Oh, yuck! The encyclopedia of everything nasty.* New York: Workman.
McDonald, M. (2002). *Judy moody.* Cambridge, MA: Candlewick.
McPhail, D. (1997). *Edward and the pirates.* New York: Little, Brown.
Mead, A. (1997). *Junebug.* New York: Dell Yearling.
Mitchell, M. (1993). *Gone with the wind.* New York: Warner Books.

References

Nimmo, J. The *Charlie Bones* series. New York: Orchard.

Nixon, J. L. (1987). *A family apart.* New York: Bantam Doubleday Dell.

Nixon, J. L. (1987). *The other side of dark.* New York: Laurel Leaf.

Ohkami, M., Ichimura, Y., & DeMarle, M. (2002). *Dragon knights.* Los Angeles: TokyoPop.

Paolini, C. (2005). *Eldest.* New York: Alfred A. Knopf.

Paolini, C. (2004). *Eragon.* New York: Knopf Books for Young Readers.

Paterson, K. (2002). *The same stuff as stars.* New York: HarperTrophy.

Perkins, L. R. (2005). *Criss cross.* New York: HarperCollins.

Philbrick. R. (2000). *The last book in the universe.* New York: Scholastic.

Philbrick, R. (2004). *The young man and the sea.* New York: Scholastic.

Pringle, L. (1997). *An extraordinary life: The story of a monarch butterfly.* Fremont, CA: Orchard.

Quindlen, A. (2004). *Imagined London.* Washington, DC: National Geographic Society.

Randle, K. D. (1996). *The only alien on the planet.* New York: Scholastic.

Raskin, E. (1978). *The westing game.* New York: Penguin.

Robinson, M. (2004). *Gilead.* New York: Farrar, Straus & Giroux.

Roy, R. (1998). *The empty envelope.* New York: Random House Books for Young Readers.

Sachar, L. (1998). *Holes.* New York: Dell Yearling.

Sebestyen, O. (1994). *Out of nowhere.* New York: Puffin.

Shusterman, N. (2004). *The schwa was here.* New York: Dutton Children's Books.

Snicket, L. The *A Series of Unfortunate Events* series. New York: HarperCollins.

Soto, G. (2003). *The afterlife.* New York: Harcourt.

Spinelli, J. (1996). *Crash.* New York: Knopf.

Spinelli, J. (1990). *Maniac magee.* New York: Little Brown.

Spinelli, J. (2000). *Stargirl.* New York: Alford A. Knopf.

Stilton, G. (2004). *Geronimo Stilton #9: A fabumouse vacation for Geronimo.* New York: Scholastic.

Weir, A. (1999). *The life of Elizabeth I.* New York: Ballantine.

Weston, C. The *Melanie Martin* series. New York: Dell Yearling.

Weston, C. (2000). *The diary of Melanie Martin or how I survived Matt the brat, Michelangelo, and the leaning tower of pizza.* New York: Dell Yearling.

Winthrop, E. (1986). *The castle in the attic.* New York: Dell Yearling.

Wright, B. R. (1995). *The dollhouse murders.* New York: Scholastic.

Movies Cited

Hughes, J. (Director). (1986). Ferris Bueller's Day Off. [Motion Picture] United States: Paramount Pictures.

Robinson, P. A. (Director). (1989). Field of Dreams. [Motion picture] United States: Universal Studios.

Index

Accountability
    teachers and, 64–65
Allington, Richard L.
    reading achievement and access to books, 22
    reading engagement, 44
Amber Brown [book series], 76, 87
Animorphs [book series], 67–69

Bailey School Kids [book series], 89
Balanced literacy classroom. *See also Supported independent reading.*
    supported independent reading in the, 4–6
Beers, Kylene
    library environment, struggling readers' view of, 44
Bloom, Becky
    Wolf!, 50
Books I Want to Read sheet
    example of, 127
    as a monitoring tool for student reading, 51

Book pass sheet
    example of, 125
    as a student library guide, 46–47
Brownlee, S.
    research on brain development, 85

Caine, Renate Nummela & Caine, Geoffrey
    downshifting of thinking, 84–85
    relaxed alertness concept and student reading levels, 10–11, 115
Calkins, Lucy M.
    independent reading, conferencing during, 3, 69
    leveled libraries, 23
Carlsen, G. Robert
    "unconscious delight" of series books, 89, 107
Carver, Ronald P.
    student levels of reading achievement, teacher responsibility in guiding, 10, 11
Character clue collection chart
    examples of, 126, 128
    as a tool for character analysis, 61–62

Charlie Bones [book series], 113–114
The classroom library
    authors listed as suggestions for, 24–26
    environment for, 26
    as a resource for reading achievement, 21–23
Cleary, Beverly
    Ramona the Pest, 90–93
Connecting to the Character [chart]
    example of, 129
    as a tool for character analysis, 62

Daniels, Harvey & Bizar, Marilyn
    student choice in "best practice" classrooms, 8, 44
Deskside conferencing
    benefits of, for students, 80
    focusing of, 75–79
    issues involving, outlined, 77–79
    preparing for, 70
    purposes of, 69–70
    questions for the initiating of, 74
    structure of, components listed, 73
    student responses during, teacher assessment of, 75, 79–80
    teacher approach toward, 72, 73
    teaching content of, outlined, 70–71
    as the teaching piece of supported independent reading, xiv
    vignette of, 67–69
Dragon Knights [book series], 104

Eldest, 4, 116–117
Eragon, 115–117

Fascinating You [assignment]
    example of, 121–122
    teacher knowledge of student interests acquired through, 9
Five-finger rule
    as a strategy for student reading choices, 11–12, 78
Fountas, Irene C. & Pinnell, Gay Su
    advanced-level texts, components of, 102
    independent reading, conferencing during, 3

Gallagher, M. C. & Pearson, P. David
    guided release model of instruction, 4, 30
Geronimo Stilton [book series], 94–96
Guided reading. *See also Supported independent reading.*
    supported independent reading and, comparison of, 7
    teacher involvement in, 6
    teacher views on the importance of, 19–20
Guthrie, John T. & Knowles, K. T.
    student choice and motivation in learners, 8

Harry Potter [book series], 37

Independence
    teacher encouragement and support of in students, 3–4
Independent reading. *See also Supported Independent reading.*
    as activity, 1–3
    conferencing during, 3
    importance of time for, 19–20
    as instructional tool, 1

Jensen, Eric
    brain research on stress, results of, 20
    brain research on student learning, 31
    learned helplessness, prevention of, 79–80
Jobe, R. & Dayton-Sakari, M.
    reading choice, the power of, 49

Keene, Ellin O. & Zimmermann, Susan
    metacognitive readers, 60
    proficient reading strategies highlighted by, 56, 59

Lesesne, Teri S.
    appropriate reading selection, importance of, 11, 103

graduating high school teachers, attitudes of toward reading, 102
reading autobiographically, 107
Library books. *See also* The classroom library.
    student expectations and the selection of, 44–45
    student selection of, teacher questions for, 12–13, 15
        outlined, 14
    teacher–student preparation for library time, 15–16
Lyon, George Ella
    Book, 50
    A Sign, 50
Lyons, Carol A.
    reading motivation, research on, 50

Maniac Magee, 112
McKenna, Michael C.
    classroom reading culture and student motivation, 21–22, 50
    student engagement with text, factors shaping, 42
    student expectations and motivation to read, 9, 44
McPhail, David
    Edward and the Pirates, 50
Melanie Martin [book series], 76, 87–89
Mossflower, 4

Note taking
    characteristics of, for effectiveness in, 57–58
    choosing a focus for, 58–59
    as opposed to worksheets, 59–60
    sticky notes, use of, 61
    by teachers, 34
        sample of, 124
    as a tool for teacher assessment of student reading, 57

Orphan Train [book series], 55

"Plot Mountain" [poster]
    as a guide for reading, 95
    illustration of, 132

Ramona Quimby [book series], 4, 76, 115
Read alouds
    chapter recommendations for, 47
    as necessary for reading engagement, 50
    as preparation for character analysis, 62
Reader(s)
    book trader(s) [type of], reading habits of, 103
    conferencing with, vignette, 103–105
    building the concept of, 38–42
    delayed [type of], defined, 83–84
        behaviors of, 85–86
        strategies for motivation of, 96–99
        understanding the, 84–85
    expectations of for reading, 44–45
        lessons aimed at changing of, 45–49
    gifted [type of], invisibility of to teachers, 111
        appropriate reading levels for, 112
        book selections for, listed, 114
        teaching points in conferences with, outlined, 117–118
    helpless [type of], conferencing with, 86–89
        vignette on, 87–89
    history as (a), 43
    ideas on, listed, 42
    lingering [type of], 115
        conference with, vignette, 115–117
    on-level [type of], lack of focus on, 101–102
        needs of, 102–103, 107–109
        teaching points for conferences with, 108–109
    page turner(s) [type of], 106

conference with, vignette, 106–107
redefining the term of, 38
response of, 55
   developing abilities for, 56
   talk as a, 64
smoke and mirrors [type of], qualities of, 90
   conference with, vignette, 90–93
speeding [type of], 112–113
   conference with, vignette, 112–113
starving [type of], needs of, 94
   conference with, vignette, 94–96
strategies used by, 60
struggling [type of], defined, 83–84
types of, xiv

Reading log(s)
   sample of, 27, 123
   value as assessment tools for teachers, 27–28
Routman, Regie
   reading achievement and access to books, 22
   reading essentials, focus on, 56

Sachar, Louis
   Holes, 113–114
Shared reading
   teacher control in, 5
Snicket, Lemony
   A Series of Unfortunate Events [book series], 104–105
SSR (sustained silent reading)
   model, and independent reading, 2
Supported independent reading. *See also Independent reading.*
   in the balanced literary classroom, 4–6
      levels of teacher support for, illustrated, 5
   benefits of, xiv, 36
   classroom culture and, 50–51
   guided reading and, differences between, 6, 7

   comparison of, illustrated, 7
   impact of on student reading, 19–20
   the minilesson and, 30–31
      sample of and strategies for, 31–32
      three purposes of, 31
   purpose of, xiv, 36, 112
   reading logs for, 27–28
   self-selected texts for, 7–10
   structure of, 20
   student choice for, and reading growth, 10–12
   student response and, 35, 55–56, 60–63
      creation of, 63–64
      targeted conferencing for, 33–34
      teacher note taking and, 34
      sample of, 124
   teacher expectations for, 28–30
   the teacher's role in, 6–7, 10–12, 16–17, 21, 35–36, 48–49, 50–51

T-chart
   examples of, 130–131
   as a tool for character analysis, 62, 63
Tomlinson, Carol
   student entitlement, 101

Venn diagram
   as a graphic organizer for creating student responses to reading, 63
Vygotsky, Lev S.
   actual level of [reading] development and student attitudes toward reading, 63
   learning as monitored by knowledgeable other, 2
   Thought and Language, 11
   zone of proximal development, 2, 73

Worthy, J.
   student choice and positive attitudes toward reading, 8

About the Author

In her 22 years as a public school teacher, Nancy Allison has worked at the high school, middle school, and intermediate school levels. For 18 of those 22 years, she has been in a highly diverse urban setting where she has worked with English language learners from around the world as well as learners from economically challenged, highly mobile families. It was here that she developed her strong belief in gearing instruction to meet the needs of each individual learner as she worked to find ways to help each student in her classroom develop a true love for both reading and for writing. She has helped develop and present graduate-level courses in balanced literacy, regularly presents staff development workshops on both reading and writing, and has presented at conferences around the country. She is currently the language arts school improvement specialist at Spring Woods Middle School in the Spring Branch Independent School District in Houston, Texas.